THE BEGINNER'S GUIDE TO

fixing your PC

HOW TO SOLVE THE COMMONEST COMPUTER PROBLEMS

 Software Installation

 Error Messages

 Malware

 Hardware Solutions

Crashes and Viruses

PETE NEALE
GEOFF STEVENS

THE BEGINNER'S GUIDE TO FIXING YOUR PC

Summersdale Publishers Ltd
46 West Street
Chichester
West Sussex
PO19 1RP
UK

www.summersdale.com

Printed and bound in Great Britain

ISBN: 978-1-84024-596-7

Acknowledgements

All screenshots and images reprinted by kind permission. WinZip screenshot copyright © WinZip International LLC. This material is the copyrighted work of WinZip International LLC. WinZip is a registered trademark of WinZip International LLC. All rights reserved.

BIOS screenshot copyright © Phoenix Technologies Ltd. Spybot screenshot copyright © Safer-Networking Ltd. AdAware screenshot copyright © Lavasoft AB.

To my mother, who taught me how to read, and to Stan Lee, who taught me not to dumb it down
Pete Neale

Contents

Introduction

For 90 per cent of the computer problems you'll ever encounter, you don't have to be an expert programmer or an electrical engineer to fix them. Once you know a few basics, you can solve most of the problems yourself. Best of all, there's no real trick to it.

All you need to know is a few simple things about your computer and how it works, and a few techniques for figuring out what's wrong. When you're driving your car and the fuel light or the oil light comes on, you know what to do straight away. If a strange light shaped like a donkey on a skateboard lights up you may have no idea what it means, but you'd probably know enough to grab the manual out of the glove compartment and look it up. If the car just won't start you can always open up the bonnet and check for broken hoses, loose battery leads or anything else obvious. Only when you've exhausted everything you know about car maintenance do you phone up a recovery service and ask for someone to fix it for you.

Computer problems are much the same. When they're fixing your computer, what those technical support people don't tell you is that they're not geniuses who know everything there is to know about computers. Mostly they've just seen the problem lots of times before and, if they haven't, they know how to check the basics to figure out what the problem might be and where to look for a solution. Given the number of computer users these days, the odds are very good that someone else has had your problem before.

That is what this book is all about. It will show you what symptoms to look for, how to do basic problem diagnosis and where to look to find a solution. It won't teach you how to program or rewire circuit boards, or turn you into a computer guru. But it will show you how to fix the most common problems you'll encounter, and introduce you to basic techniques for solving other problems not covered in these pages. Hopefully, by the time you've finished reading this book, you'll be able to fix most of your problems yourself without having to ring a helpline and listen to Vivaldi for half an hour at 50 pence per minute.

WHAT'S IN THIS BOOK, AND WHAT'S NOT

This book is not a list of answers to every possible computer problem: that's obviously not realistic.

We do provide a lot of suggestions for many common problems. For most of the problems you'll encounter you should manage to find the answer you want or at least something close enough so you can figure the rest out yourself.

But what if you hit a problem we haven't specifically covered? That's why a large section of this book is devoted to showing you the tips, techniques and general philosophy of problem solving we use day to day. Armed with this know-how you can learn to solve your problems like the Technical Support Masters do.

Finally, the Fixing Your PC Before It Breaks section gives tips and advice on how to avoid problems in the first place, or at least ensure that when something serious does go wrong you can manage to put things back to how they were before.

How to read this book

This book was not designed to be read from cover to cover. If you're reading this you either have a problem already, or you don't. So... if you have a problem:

- First check the contents and index to see if your problem matches anything listed there. If so, that's great and it's worth the price of the book in itself.

- No luck? The book is divided into problem areas: hardware, software and so on. So try to decide which one your problem falls under. Read the introduction at the start of each section to see if it's relevant. You may learn more about the type of problem you're dealing with and possible avenues to explore for solving it.

- Still stumped? Try Chapter Two. Hopefully, this will help you identify the problem so you can find out how to fix it. Almost every problem has been found by someone before you. One thing you can count on with geeks: they love to solve problems and then post the solution on a web page so others can benefit (and see how clever they are). So if you can identify what's wrong, you can almost certainly find a solution somewhere on the Internet.

Introduction

- You don't have a problem yet? Great, try and keep it that way if you can. Read through Chapter One, which will help you avoid problems arising. An ounce of prevention is worth a pound of cure. Then read on into the rest of the book, for tips and techniques to deal with problems as they arise.

Chapter One:
Fixing Your PC Before It Breaks

It's probably best to get the bad news out of the way first.

Your PC will break one day. It's not what anyone wants to hear, but unfortunately it's true. If you're very lucky, you'll stop using it before that day comes. If you're unlucky, it will happen just after you finished cataloguing your collection of 100,000 butterflies in a database. But it will happen. Nothing in life is certain, except for death, taxes and PC failure.

Now, it's obviously not possible to fix something that's not actually broken yet. However, there is a lot you can do before it breaks to put that day off for as long as possible, and to make it as painless as possible when it does eventually arrive.

Like most accidents, most PC problems are avoidable with a little planning and forethought. In this chapter we give you advice on how to avoid potential problems and prepare your PC to make things easier to put right.

Section 1:
Back up, back up, back up

We can't say it often enough: back up, back up, back up.

Your PC consists of hardware, the stuff you can touch (because it's hard), software, the stuff you can't touch (because it isn't hard) and your valuable data, which you gathered while you were using the computer. The hardware and software (both systems software like Windows and applications like Word) can all be replaced, sometimes at a price. However, you may be unable to replace your data at any price.

So – back up, back up, back up.

By back up, we mean make a copy of the stuff you have that's important. If your computer is catastrophically broken, you may have to start again with a new computer. If your valuable data exists only on the inaccessible disk of your broken computer you face the choice of either losing it altogether, or trying to recover the data off the disk. Recovering data is often difficult to organise, expensive, ultimately impossible or all three. If your valuable data exists somewhere else (a backup), at least you can put it back on your new PC. That's what backups are for.

The world of ICT is littered with the corpses of technical people who didn't make good backups of their data and paid the price for it. With more than sixty years' combined experience in the computer business, the single most important lesson we've learned is to back up important stuff. So back up, bac... well, you probably have the idea now.

What should you back up?

First, you have to decide what your valuable data is. It might be all your photographs, your correspondence, your contacts, your music, your business accounts, even your collection of vintage computer hardware brochure scans. Only you can decide what your valuable data is, because only you know what you use your PC for.

It can be hard to work out where your data is on your disk. On Windows, a good starting point is your home directories. These are where you'll find My Documents, My Pictures and the like. In Windows, these can all be found on your C drive in a folder called Documents and Settings/YourLoginID. For example, if you log on to Windows as Pete, then it would be in Documents and Settings/Pete. In Vista, they're in Users/Pete.

That's fine for documents you create yourself. However, an application may save data in its own special folder. The Internet is your friend (or at least a well-meaning acquaintance) and some research starting with the name of the program you use to get at the data will usually give you some good pointers. Try looking for the information on the application's website, or try typing 'Where does Filemaker database store its data?' into Google (assuming Filemaker database is the name of the application). Someone out there has almost certainly asked before. If your application's website has a forum or discussion board, then sign up and simply ask the question. Someone will answer in a day or five.

When should you back up?

Now! Go on, we'll wait. Done? Good, we'll continue.

Backups should be done regularly. How often depends on how much your data changes. If your data changes often, you may want to back up daily. If it's vitally important to your business, maybe more often. If it changes less often, you may find that weekly or even monthly suits you. A good way to look at it is to ask yourself how much effort it would take to replace the data from scratch, i.e.

how much work would you lose. A few hours to re-create lost data might be fine, but if it would take you days then you're not backing up often enough. On the other hand, if you spend time every day backing up stuff that would only take a few minutes to recreate, you're either backing up too often, or the wrong stuff.

EXPERT TIP

Keep old copies of your backups. If you keep the most recent backup and the previous two, then you also guard against something being wrong with one of the backups, or from deleting a file so it's no longer backed up, and then discovering much later you still want it. For example, we use a scheme along the lines of doing a daily backup which we keep for a week, a weekly backup which we keep for a month, and a monthly backup which we keep for a year.

What should you back up to?

We recommend CDs or DVDs, as these are cheap, reliable and easy to transport.

You might also consider external hard drives (computer disks attached to your PC by a USB or FireWire connection). These are bulkier and more prone to failure, but can hold a lot more data than a DVD.

An internal hard drive (like a D drive on your computer) can be quick and hold a lot of data, but is not really recommended because you're only protecting your data against your other drive failing.

If you have more than one computer on your network, you can back each one up to the other. This can be reasonably quick and effective, and if the computers are in two different locations, very safe indeed.

You may wish to research online backups: these services, available for a small fee, let you send your data over the Internet to a 'digital safe'. Your ISP may provide a service for free or at a nominal cost (e.g. BT's Digital Vault). If you're thinking about online backup, consider the reliability of the service as you're trusting those people to look after your data.

Backing up to tapes is unlikely to be cost effective or reliable for the home user.

EXPERT TIP

Test your backups.

Another important point is to test you can restore the data before you need to do it because of a catastrophe. Many times we've heard of people, even highly-paid IT professionals, who have been let down by backups they didn't test before catastrophe struck.

Where should you store your backups?

That largely depends on how paranoid you are and how valuable the data is to you.

The best place is a different physical location. Then if your house burns down or the nearby power sub-station gets struck by lightning and the electrical surge fries your PC, you're still OK. You can take a CD, DVD or external hard drive to the office or stick them in the boot of your car and feel pretty safe. Online backup services are by definition somewhere else, so you don't need to worry about transporting stuff around.

Please remember also that your valuable data may contain information which personally identifies you. When you back it up, make sure you don't leave it lying around for anyone to pick up, or you may find yourself the victim of identity theft.

Backing up your system and applications

Microsoft Windows XP and Vista PCs have a system backup feature. This doesn't back up your data, but it does back up the Windows system and your applications. Better yet, by default Windows does it automatically whenever it changes something on your system.

If you like to install a lot of applications on your computer (especially ones you've downloaded off the Internet), and plugging in new hardware, you can easily break the system. So before you make any changes along these lines, you can also create your own system backups at any point. If you want to create a system backup (a 'Restore Point') you have to find **System Restore** (see Fig. 1 or Fig. 2 for Vista) and select the **Create a Restore Point** option (see Fig. 5).

System Restore

If you've just installed a new piece of hardware or software and you're experiencing serious problems, this feature will let you roll your system and applications (mostly) back to where they were before you changed things. To get to System Restore, click **Start**, **All Programs**, **Accessories**, **System Tools**, and **System Restore** (see Fig. 1 or Fig. 2 for Vista). Here, you can choose to back up or restore your system.

If you choose to restore, you then pick the date you'll restore from (see Fig. 3 or Fig. 4 for Vista) and which particular backup if you made more than one that day. All programs and hardware drivers you've installed since that date will magically disappear. And so, hopefully, will the problem.

If your PC is so broken it won't even boot to the normal Desktop, you may be able to get it into Safe Mode or boot from a CD (see Safe Mode, Section 4 of this chapter).

It's often best to run System Restore from Safe Mode anyway, especially if you're trying to roll back hardware changes.

The bad news about System Restore is that it doesn't always work. If it doesn't, you may be looking at a system reinstall, or perhaps you have a hardware problem.

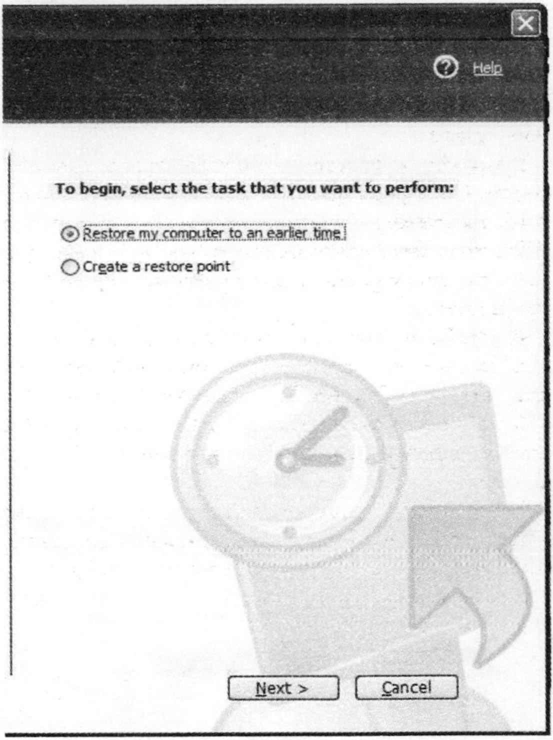
Help
To begin, select the task that you want to perform:
Restore my computer to an earlier time
Create a restore point
Next >
Cancel

Fig. 1

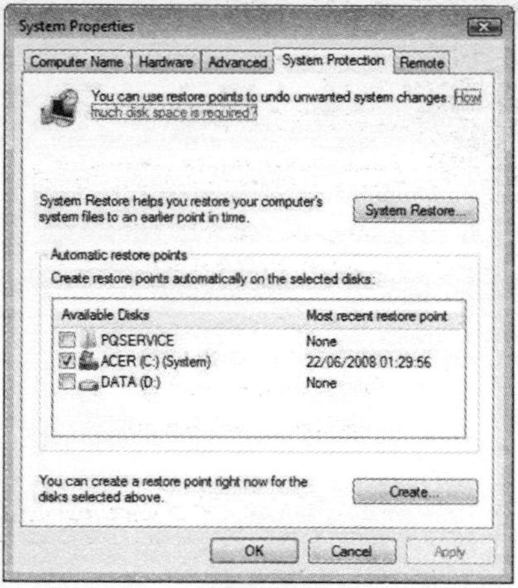
System Properties
Computer Name
Hardware
Advanced
System Protection
Remote
You can use restore points to undo unwanted system changes. How much disk space is required?
System Restore helps you restore your computer's system files to an earlier point in time.
System Restore...
Automatic restore points
Create restore points automatically on the selected disks:
Available Disks
Most recent restore point
PQSERVICE
None
ACER (C:) (System)
22/06/2008 01:29:56
DATA (D:)
None
You can create a restore point right now for the disks selected above.
Create...
OK
Cancel
Apply

Fig. 2

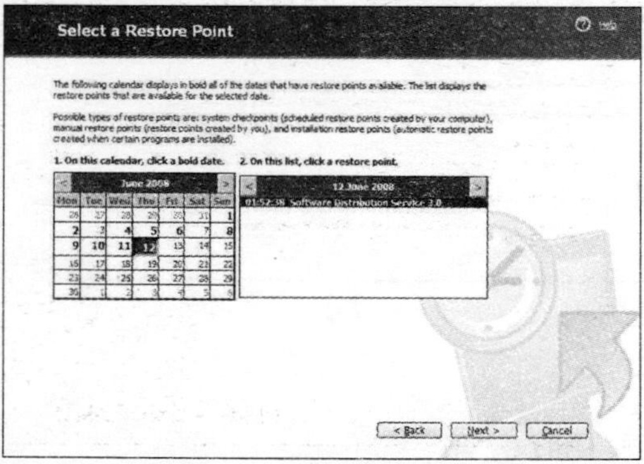
Select a Restore Point
The following calendar displays in bold all of the dates that have restore points available. The list displays the restore points that are available for the selected date.
Possible types of restore points are: system checkpoints (scheduled restore points created by your computer), manual restore points (restore points created by you), and installation restore points (automatic restore points created when certain programs are installed).
1. On this calendar, click a bold date.
2. On this list, click a restore point.
June 2008
12 June 2008
01:52:38 Software Distribution Service 3.0
< Back
Next >
Cancel

Fig. 3

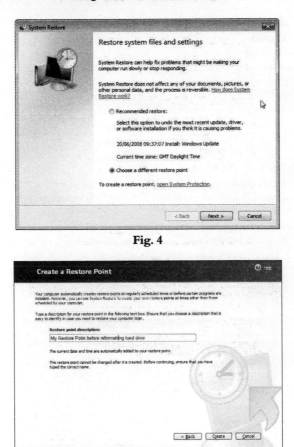

Fig. 4

Fig. 5

Backing up data

Because System Restore might not help you out, and because your problems may not just be software ones, you still need to back up your valuable data so you can recreate it on a new computer.

These days, your valuable data almost always includes details of how you use online services, user IDs and passwords. Remember, you may have to back those details up too.

There are a wide variety of ways to back up your data. The simplest is to copy the data to the CD (or whatever you're backing up to) using copy and paste or drag and drop in Windows Explorer. This method is simple, but it can use up a lot of CD space.

We recommend using a product which compresses the data to a much smaller size. This means it fits on fewer CDs, or takes less time to upload to an online backup service. There are a number of products which do this, from the ever popular WinZip to products like WinRar and 7Zip (see Useful Resources).

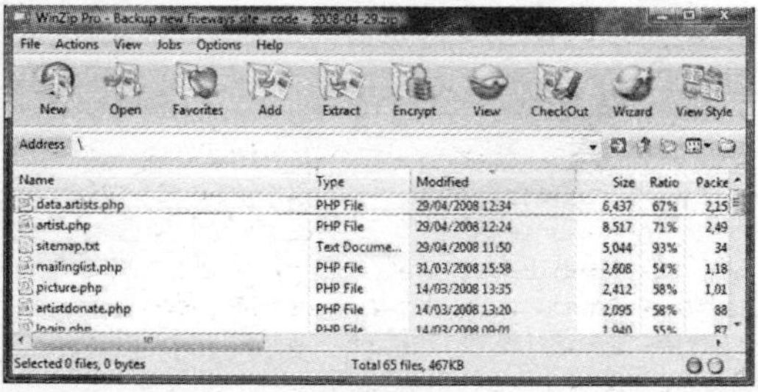

Fig. 6

If you really want to, there are any number of expensive backup software packages you could invest in. These can automatically run the backups for you at certain times, include and exclude files and folders, copy the backup files hither and yon and all sorts of other bells and whistles. If you're having trouble setting up a backup regime with something like WinZip, these might help you out, but you will be paying for the privilege. Another thing to be wary of is the format these packages store the files in. If you simply copy the files or use a popular compression package, you can easily get the files back without special software (for example, Windows can read WinZip files automatically). However, if the backup software you choose has its own way of storing the data, you may well need a working version of their software if you want to access your backed-up data.

BACKUP SUMMARY

- Identify your valuable data, the stuff that's impossible or very hard work to recreate
- Back your data up regularly
- Test you can restore your data
- Don't leave your backups exposed to misuse

And one final word to the wise – you can't back up too much or too frequently. If you do, the worst you end up with is a lot of backup CDs lying around. However, if you back up too little or too seldom, you are likely to find that the backed-up version of the file you are looking for is either way out of date or missing entirely.

Finally, in case you're not entirely clear what the section on backups was about, or you skipped straight to the summary, the moral of the story is – back up, back up, back up.

Section 2:
Keep software current

Microsoft provides online updates for its operating systems and applications. So do lots of other software suppliers. We recommend you apply all the updates you can. While there's a small risk updates will cause problems, it's generally outweighed by the benefits the updates bring in terms of fixing bugs you might not have encountered yet. If you've got a problem with an application, you may find that just applying the latest update or upgrading to the latest version is the answer. And if you go looking for support from the supplier of a program, the first thing they'll ask is 'Have you applied the latest updates?'. If you haven't, they'll tell you to go and do it and see if it solves the problem. So you might as well do it regularly yourself and save the cost of a ten-minute support call. Microsoft and many other suppliers enable you to do this automatically.

You can usually choose an option which will allow you to download the changes and review them before deciding exactly which updates you want installed. You should consider doing this as you may have a good reason for not wanting to update some software automatically. It's always a good idea to know what changes are being made to your system before they actually happen, and you might want to have a particular version of some software on your machine. One reason not to upgrade software is because your employer says so (unreasonable, maybe, but not uncommon).

To set up Windows for automatic updates, click on **Start**, then **Control Panel**, then select **Automatic Updates** (see Fig.7 or Fig. 8 for Vista). You can turn this on or off, or set it up to check but ask for permission to install the updates. For other applications, you can usually find an option in the menu under **Tools**, **Help**, **Options** or similar where you can tick a box to choose to look for updates automatically.

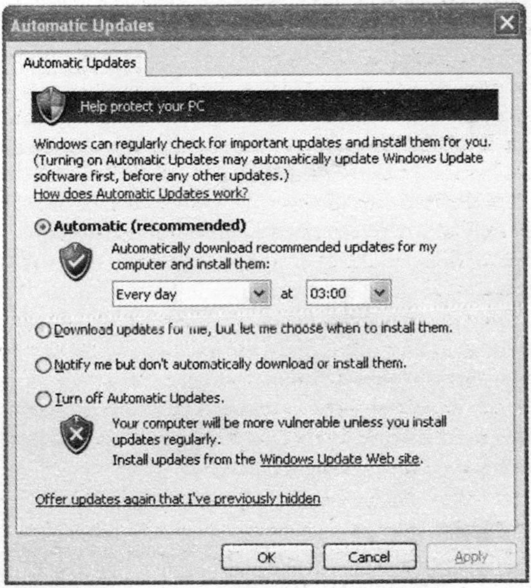

Fig. 7

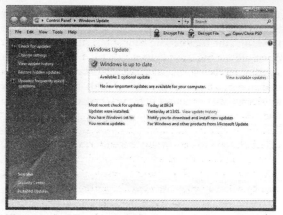

Fig. 8

You may also have to hunt down the latest versions of some of your application programs on the Internet. As always, make sure you're downloading the program from a website you trust (see Security). If you do have to check a website to find out if there are updates and are the sort of person who always forgets, you can use a web facility like ChangeDetection (www.changedetection.com), which offers a free facility to check a web page daily and notify you by email of any time it changes.

Section 3: Security

Security isn't our primary focus in this book, but we have to mention some aspects of it, because today your PC can be broken by people who aren't even on the same continent as you.

Surfing the Internet can be just like surfing the ocean. Sometimes a big wave comes along and bowls you over ('getting worked over' for real surfers). If you're lucky, you come up breathing on the other side of it. That big wave working you over on the Internet is people who want to run your computer remotely, without your knowledge, or steal your identity to enrich themselves and leave you to explain the bill written in your name. If you'd rather be on a shady recliner on the beach with a cool drink in your hand, you need to think about online security. Otherwise, these rogues will gain access to your PC and break it for you.

There's no one measure that makes your computer secure. The most important part of your PC security is you. Don't blindly download and install things. It's important to understand what you're downloading, and to think about where you're downloading it from. All kinds of viruses, malware (software that does BAD things) and rogue software are freely downloadable on the Internet if you're unwary enough to agree to the attractive dialog box. Many will try and fool you by saying things like 'You have a virus, click here to remove it'. Click there and you will have a virus. Some try and fool you by appearing to be from a friend. One virus will send a message to you via MSN from one of your contacts, encouraging you to look at a picture of them. Click at your own risk. So a good rule of thumb is never download, accept or run anything that you did not specifically go looking for from a source you know and trust, or can at least verify in some way. And always scan anything for viruses before you run it.

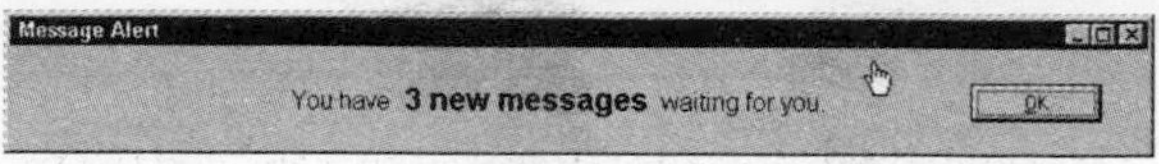

Fig. 9

Similarly, you will receive enticing emails inviting you to install their attachments or click their links. Don't do that. Any email with an attachment from someone you don't know is not just probably unwanted, but also suspicious. There's a quick, easy way to protect yourself when you receive any email from someone you don't know. It's called the Delete key.

Lots of us keep details about our lives on our PCs. Many people's PCs are like filing cabinets containing their important documents. Increasingly, we're all making transactions online, accessing shopping websites, using financial services like online banking, ordering pizzas and so on. If other people are accessing your PC they can install all kinds of untrustworthy software on it. Microsoft Windows is getting better and better at isolating users from each other, but there are plenty of other people trying to defeat that isolation, and no security system is so good it can't be broken (and many are so bad they might as well not exist). When you're making transactions online you should try to use the computer you trust the most. Ideally, use a computer only you use, and have all the security measures in place that are recommended in this book.

If you're accessing sensitive sites – doing online banking or supplying information like your credit card details for a purchase, for example – it's safer to have just one browser window open at the time. Browsers aren't supposed to leak information between different pages they display, but a huge number of malware writers are trying to find ways to do just that. Because of the complexity of modern browsers, they often succeed.

EXPERT TIP

If you make online purchases, consider opening a special bank account and/or credit card exclusively for online use. Keep the balances small, and overdraft/credit limits small. Then if someone does steal your details, they can't spend that much. If the account is with your regular bank, when you make a large purchase you can transfer the necessary money online from your regular account to cover it.

Anti-virus

You MUST have a working anti-virus program installed on your computer. Even if your PC isn't connected to the Internet, viruses and other malware continue to pop up on all known digital media. You must update your anti-virus software frequently, so it knows about the latest viruses. Most anti-virus software can be set up to check automatically for new updates every day. If you're not connected to the Internet, you'll need to obtain CDs from a manufacturer.

There are a lot of anti-virus programs around that you can use. Most PCs will come with a free trial of Norton or McAfee anti-virus software already installed. These products generally require a yearly subscription fee to get the daily updates. You will need to subscribe to these – anti-virus software which isn't updated regularly is a waste of time because new viruses are being created all the time.

If you prefer not to pay, there are a couple of free anti-virus programs you can install. These products generally make their money by having a basic free product, and a much more advanced version they sell to people who want more security and businesses that want to protect lots of PCs. AVG Free (see Useful Resources) is a good example of a free anti-virus program and can be recommended for most basic home PC users.

However, if you do go for a free product and not one of the big names like Norton or McAfee, it's usually best to get a recommendation from a friend who already uses it. Unknown software is always a big risk and unknown anti-virus software is just begging for trouble.

Firewall

If you're online you MUST have a working firewall between you and the Internet, which is connected to nearly every other computer in the world.

Your PC is like a building with literally thousands of doors opening into it. The Internet, and any local network you have, is a very busy road that passes all the doors. A real building has locks on the doors to keep out passing rogues, and a firewall to stop the flames and heat spreading when the neighbour's house burns down. A computer has locks on the doors to keep out those who wish you harm and a firewall to stop things spreading as well, but it's all bundled together and called a firewall. The firewall determines which doors are locked and which will open to any passer-by, and its purpose is to stop bad things passing from other PCs to yours.

Most PCs come with some kind of firewall built in. You can find it listed in the Control Panel under Windows Firewall. If it's not turned on for some reason, turn it on now. Most broadband connections use a router to connect you to the Internet and most routers also come with a firewall built in. It's a good idea to make sure the router firewall and the firewall on your PC are both turned on.

You can also invest in a proprietary firewall. Most companies that deal in Internet security offer firewalls as well as anti-virus software. On the whole, for the average home user, the Windows and router firewalls are more than sufficient. If you're wearing belt and braces already, you probably don't need to tie a rope around your waist as well, but there is nothing to stop you using a proprietary firewall if you so desire.

Configuring firewalls can be a complicated business, especially for the casual user. As a general rule, firewalls are set up to allow almost nothing into your PC, which is what you want. You may find that some applications, like games which you play with other users on the Internet, want to open a port (unlock a door) in your firewall. They can generally do this automatically, but when you run a program for the first time your firewall may pop up a box saying that the application is trying to open a port. If the application is a well-known program from a respectable company, and has a good reason for wanting to do it (like a multi-user game), then go ahead and allow it to open the port. If it's not a well-known program, think twice. If you can't think of a good reason why the DVD-viewing program you downloaded from www.freesoftware4you.com is trying to open a port, don't allow it until you've done some research. A quick visit to Google and a search on 'Why is EvilDVDViewer opening a port?' will usually net you a fair few pages. Don't trust the first one you look at – check several and see if there's a consensus of opinion.

Unfortunately, firewalls can cause some problems as well (see Section 3: Internet and Networking in Chapter Four).

Shared files

Shared files and folders are a good way to pass data to other programs on your local network. You can share a folder by right-clicking on the folder in Windows Explorer and selecting **Share** or **Sharing and Security** (see Fig. 10 or Fig. 11 and Fig. 12 for Vista). Shared folders can either be read only (other people can look but not change anything), or read/write (in which case they can do anything they want).

If you're sharing files, it's a good idea to check what your computer looks like from another PC in the network. It's very unwise to let other people write to the whole of your C drive, and it's not a good idea to let them read the whole thing. If you want to share files, make sure you only share one or a handful of folders. Windows provides a shared folder for you in its default set-up. In XP it's called Shared Documents, while in Vista it's Public Documents. One good option if you want to share files is to copy whatever it is you want to share to these folders. That way you're not exposing any other files on your computer by accident and, if someone else does delete or corrupt a file, you've still got the original you copied into the shared folder in the first place.

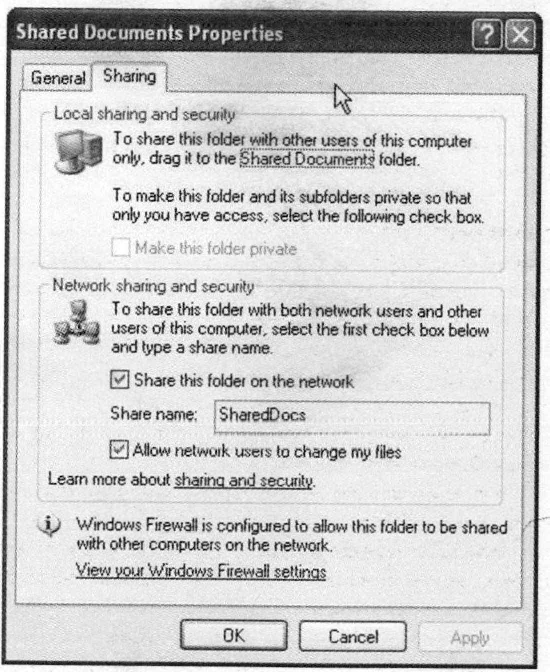

Shared Documents Properties

General | Sharing

Local sharing and security

To share this folder with other users of this computer only, drag it to the Shared Documents folder.

To make this folder and its subfolders private so that only you have access, select the following check box.

☐ Make this folder private

Network sharing and security

To share this folder with both network users and other users of this computer, select the first check box below and type a share name.

☑ Share this folder on the network

Share name: SharedDocs

☑ Allow network users to change my files

Learn more about sharing and security.

ⓘ Windows Firewall is configured to allow this folder to be shared with other computers on the network.

View your Windows Firewall settings

[OK] [Cancel] [Apply]

Fig. 10

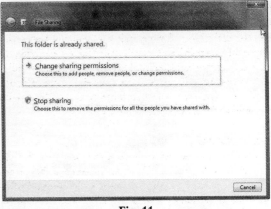

Fig. 11

Fig. 12

Wireless networks

Wireless technology advances at a breakneck pace, and so does the technology for bypassing its security and letting people into your PC and its valuable data. As we write, the most secure wireless technology uses something called WPA encryption. If you've had a wireless network for a couple of years now, you may need to think about what it's using and whether you still trust it.

Passwords

Use the longest passwords you can bear to. Really, fourteen letters, upper and lower case, and numbers is the minimum. Don't use pets, relatives, birthdays and other common or easily guessable things. Don't reuse passwords for different services.

How do you remember all your passwords? It's a real problem. We've heard notebooks, letter codes in paperback books, mobile phones and USB memory sticks proposed. We prefer something unconnected to your, or any other, computer. It should look quite unlike a list of passwords unless you're sure you have physical control of whatever it's written on.

EXPERT TIP

If you can think of a phrase you can remember easily, then you can use an acronym of it as a pretty secure password. For example, a10gh26gandaBFH (a 10 gallon hat, 2 six-guns and a Big Fat Horse).

Clearing caches

As you surf the Internet, your browser keeps copies of things it downloads and sites you visit on your hard drive in what is called a cache. Maybe you keep personal details of your life in your emails, or you opt to have your browser remember passwords for some sites for you automatically. No matter how you use your PC, you can be sure there are bits of personal information stashed away on it somewhere in a hard-to-find place – hard to find for you, anyway, not necessarily for experts who know what they're doing.

If you let your PC out of your physical control, including throwing or giving it away, it's a good idea to clear this stuff out. Your browser will have a menu item somewhere to do this. In Internet Explorer it's in **Tools**, **Internet Options** and then on the **General** tab of the options pop-up window (see Fig. 13). Click on **Delete** and the box shown in Fig. 14 will pop up. Your emails and other data can be harder to find (see Email and communication and Applications in Chapter Four).

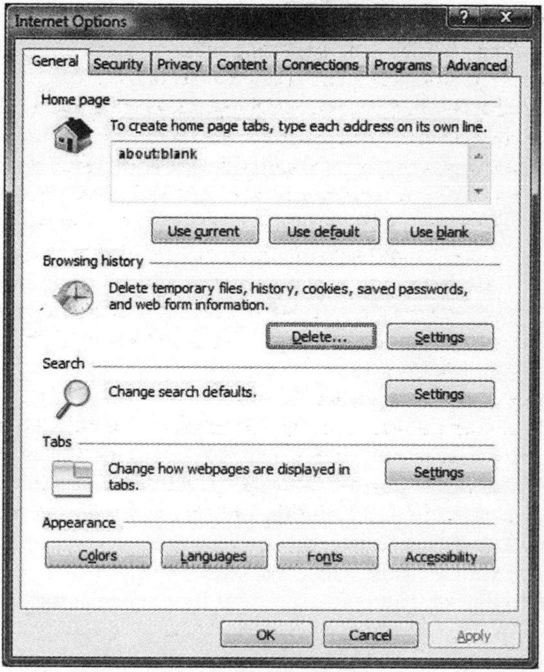
Internet Options
General
Security
Privacy
Content
Connections
Programs
Advanced
Home page
To create home page tabs, type each address on its own line.
about:blank
Use current
Use default
Use blank
Browsing history
Delete temporary files, history, cookies, saved passwords, and web form information.
Delete...
Settings
Search
Change search defaults.
Settings
Tabs
Change how webpages are displayed in tabs.
Settings
Appearance
Colors
Languages
Fonts
Accessibility
OK
Cancel
Apply

Fig. 13

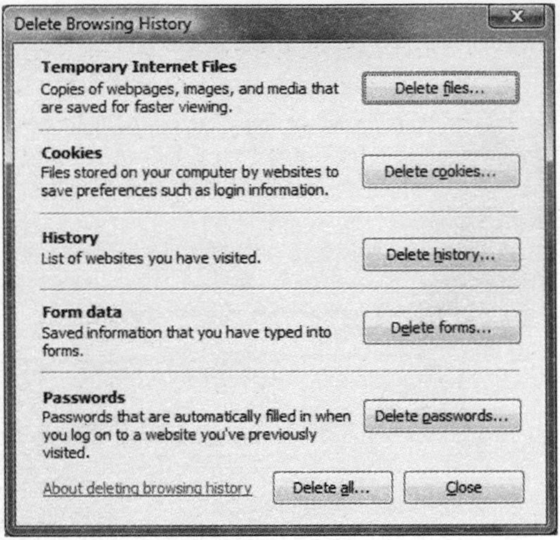

Fig. 14

If all your valuable data is backed up and you no longer need the computer, you should at least reformat the disk before you say goodbye to it. The best way to boot a utility is to do it from a CD (see Useful Resources). If you're not giving your computer away to someone who actually wants to use it, why not remove the disk after you've reformatted it and stick it in a drawer as a spare?

If you have a hardware problem and you can't access your hard drive, that doesn't mean that nobody else can. If you've got personal data you wish to keep private on a disk you can't access, the only safe thing to do is to remove the

disk from the PC or enclosure it's in (or find someone who
knows how to remove it, while you wait) and physically
destroy the disk – a hammer works well for this, but do
it outdoors and wear safety glasses and a dust mask. Or
you can mount the disk in a hard drive enclosure with a
USB interface and see if you can still read your data from
your new PC.

Section 4:
Recovery tools

Most of the time your PC is your friend: just boot it up,
sign on and start using it. Sometimes it doesn't get as far
as booting properly. You either have a hardware problem
or a serious software problem. Maybe the serious software
problem can be fixed.

WHAT DOES BOOTING MEAN?

It doesn't mean kicking your PC, no matter how much you
may be tempted to. The technical term for kicking your PC,
or whacking your TV when the reception is bad, is 'kinetic
engineering'.

When you turn on your PC, the first thing it does is run
some hardware checks, then it loads a very small program
called a bootstrap from your disk (hard drive, floppy disk, or
CD). This program is stored on a fixed place on the disk, so
the PC always knows where to look for it. If it doesn't find
the program, it will look on the next disk, until it runs out
of disks to check, at which point it will throw up its hands in
horror and die with an error message on the screen.

The bootstrap program knows about the operating system
(Windows, Linux etc.), where to find it and how to load it

---

up and start it. So the PC loads and runs the bootstrap, and the bootstrap in turn does what is necessary to run the actual operating system.

It is called a bootstrap program because some bright spark many years ago likened it to the PC hauling itself up by its own bootstraps. Over the years this whole process has been shortened to 'booting'.

Safe Mode

Microsoft Windows can be started in two ways: the normal way and Safe Mode. You can access Safe Mode by pressing F8 as you boot the computer. This starts the system with the minimum number of device drivers and other software needed to actually do something constructive. Your screen may look a little odd, but if your problem is something you just installed, you have the chance to run System Restore (see Section 1 of this chapter) and undo what you did that caused the problem.

If you're planning on running System Restore to restore anything, it's often best to run it from Safe Mode, especially if you're rolling back hardware driver changes. The less of the operating system that is active, the less chance you have of restoring something that's being used.

This may solve your problem. If you can't get to Safe Mode, or a restore doesn't help, you either have a hardware problem or a really serious software problem.

BIOS

If your PC won't boot successfully, try to get to the BIOS pages. If you can display them, you know the core of your PC is working. There's often a PC Health page where you can see the temperature of the processor and whether the fans are working. You should be able to see some indication that your PC can see your hard drive. If the hard drive is missing you definitely have a hardware problem.

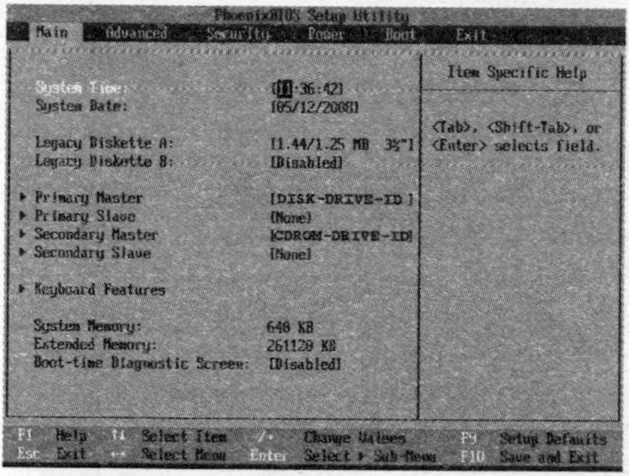

Fig. 15

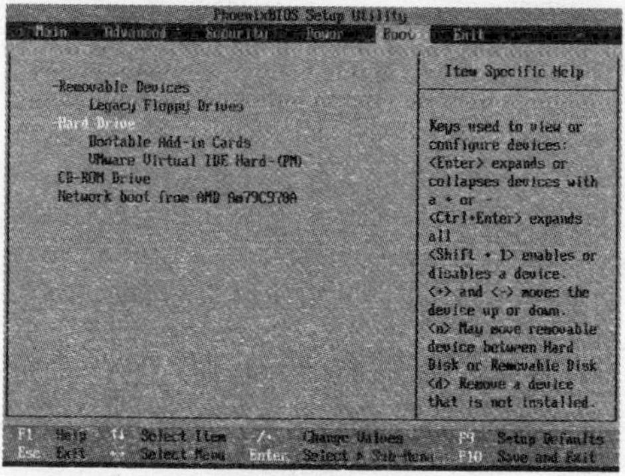

Fig. 16

WHAT'S THE BIOS?

Your PC is made of hardware and software. Between the software applications you use day to day, and the real hardware you can touch, there's a layer you rarely see called the Basic Input/Output System (BIOS). In fact, unless you go looking for it, you'll never see it. You can get access to the BIOS when you turn your PC on by holding down a special key while the PC boots up – usually Del, F2 or F8. The specific key may be mentioned in your PC documentation, and it's often shown on the screen at the very start of the boot process, usually saying something like 'Press F2 to enter Setup'. It's a good idea to find out how to do this for your PC before you need to. Don't make any changes unless you have a very good reason to and know what you're doing, but do find out how to check your PC will boot from a CD. If you've got a recent PC, you might be able to boot it from a USB stick as well as a CD. We'd like to give you precise instructions how to do this, but there are many types of BIOS, and they're not all the same.

Some laptops come with a recovery partition, which is a special part of your disk you can boot from as if it were a bootable CD. They sometimes have lots of keys to do things when you turn the power on.

If you don't have the instructions that came with your laptop or Desktop PC on what you can do with the BIOS when you turn your PC on, it's a good idea to find them on the Internet before you might need them.

Bootable CDs

Your PC may have come with a bootable CD from the manufacturer. This CD may completely reinstall Windows, possibly losing all your valuable data in the process, so check carefully exactly what it does before using it, and read all warning messages carefully.

Depending on which version of Microsoft Windows you have, your Microsoft Windows CD may be bootable, and contain useful recovery utilities. You can always try this disk to find out because it won't actually install a new Windows over your current version without at least asking you first.

It's a good idea to try and find a bootable Recovery CD for your version of Windows. At the moment it's unclear whether or not Microsoft will provide an authorised way of making your own Recovery CD for Vista, so you may have to rely on third parties. The effect of booting from the Recovery CD is similar to booting into Safe Mode.

If you're adventurous, consider downloading a Linux bootable CD, such as Knoppix. If you're faced with a PC that won't boot into Safe Mode, the Knoppix CD may boot and let you regain access to your valuable data long enough to copy it somewhere before you reinstall Windows. You will have to research and follow some slightly arcane instructions to do so. Once again, do this research before your PC goes wrong because you may not have Internet access after it dies.

Remember, you may have to set up your computer's BIOS to boot from a CD if it won't do so on the first try (See Fig. 16).

If you can't boot from the disk or any CD, your PC has a serious hardware problem and you're better off taking it to see an expert.

Spare hardware

EXPERT TIP

If you replace some piece of hardware that still functions, it's often a good idea to keep the old one as a spare. When disposing of your old PC, you can also keep any functioning components as spares.

If you have spare pluggable hardware and you're confident about swapping it, why not give it a try? We recommend marking hardware clearly before you embark on this. Keep notes about what you do. By 'pluggable hardware' we mean things like printers and keyboards. There are things inside the PC's case like hard drives that you can also replace, but you should inform yourself about the specialised knowledge and equipment you'll need before you start. There are some quite informative websites which show you step by step how to replace bits inside your PC. Be warned though, you should carefully read any manufacturer's guarantee you have before opening the case on any PC – many warranties are invalidated if you open the case.

We recommend never disassembling laptops beyond the descriptions in their user guides. The inside of a laptop is a strange and mysterious place and should only be entered by trained experts armed with tools specially blessed by the gods.

Power supplies

An uninterruptible power supply, or UPS, can be a useful addition to your PC's reliability if you suffer from utility power supply problems. Blackouts, brownouts or interference from heavy machinery can have a bad effect on your PC. A UPS may be able to smooth these bad effects out and, in a blackout, give you time to save your valuable data and shut down your PC.

If you don't want to invest in a UPS, at the very least you should get a surge protector for your wall power socket or a surge-protected multi-block if you use one. A relatively small spike in the electricity supply can fry your PC hardware. Many surge protectors also provide free insurance against equipment failure caused by the surge protector failing, and although they might not cover acts of god, a little extra free financial help when the workmen put a pickaxe through the mains supply can't go amiss.

Chapter Two:
Figuring Out Where the Problem Is

Section 1:
Narrowing it down

First, let's think about where that problem might come from. Once you have ascertained this, you can think about how to fix it. Once again, we advise you to take notes as you go through this process and review them periodically. It really does help.

The main problem most people have when trying to solve PC problems for the first time is simply not knowing where to start. It's quite daunting to sit down and try to figure out what is going wrong with your car when all you really know is you put fuel in, turn the key and it goes. With a PC you put electricity in, click with your mouse and it does stuff. Both are a bit like magic.

Solving problems is a lot like being a detective. You don't need to know a whole lot about a particular problem to start with. Conan Doyle's famous character Sherlock Holmes knew nothing about large ghostly mastiffs roaming the moors, but he did know about looking for clues, questioning suspects and eliminating possibilities. He famously said: 'When you have eliminated the impossible, whatever remains, however improbable, must be the truth.'

Solving PC problems is exactly the same, albeit without being attacked by dangerous dogs in the process. You need to look for clues (error messages, patterns in things failing, odd symptoms or behaviour of programs) and question suspects (look at log files on your PC, search the Internet for similar problems, ask the kids if they've been doing anything on your computer).

Most importantly, you've got to eliminate the impossible. In PC terms, this means thinking about what might be wrong, and trying to eliminate it as a possibility. The printer's not working. Is it plugged in? Is the fuse in the plug OK? Is it turned on? Is a cable loose? Can the PC print a test page? Can another application print anything?

Start with the simplest, most easily testable problems, partly because they're the easiest to test, and partly because most problems are caused by really basic, silly things. You'll feel really stupid if you spend days trying to fix your printer and spend money to get an expert in, only to find that he plugs the USB cable from the printer back into the PC because it was loose. So the more possibilities you can eliminate, the more specific you can make your searches on the Internet, and the more information you can give any expert to save him time checking these things. And once you've eliminated all the other possible sources of the problem, whatever remains, no matter how improbable, must be the culprit.

Section 2:
Types of problems I

Most problems fall into one of four categories:

- **Software** – a computer program goes wrong

- **Hardware** – your PC or one of the various bits and pieces attached to it – actual real things you can hold in your hands goes wrong

- **User** – you've done something to cause the problem yourself

- **DOG** – someone else did something to cause the problem

Software

Your programs won't start, or they crash. Maybe the computer won't even start properly, although the fans are whirring and the normal lights come on. Chances are, this is a software problem. Error messages when the computer is starting up or shutting down are usually to do with hardware driver errors, or just *maybe* faulty hardware. (A driver is a small program that your computer runs automatically to allow it to control a piece of hardware.)

Sometimes it can be hard to distinguish software problems from hardware problems. If your program crashes when you try to use a piece of hardware, the scanner for example, it's possible the hardware is broken. It's still more likely to be a driver problem than hardware. If your programs crash, seemingly at random, your PC's memory may be faulty. If your PC starts crashing after a period of use, it may be overheating.

The key to solving software problems is having a system with the latest versions of the software you want, and none of the software you don't want.

User

Your computer won't do what you want, despite the computer and programs starting. Maybe you're expecting the programs to do something they won't ever do, or the program is set to stop you doing it, or you're just doing something wrong. When you phone a telephone support line, the person at the other end will more than likely be assuming the problem is you. This is not a reflection on you personally, just the fact that most of the problems they have to deal with are caused by the user.

The key to solving user problems is knowledge. You need to understand what your programs actually do and how to configure them.

DOG

This stands for 'Dogs and other gremlins' (such as children and visiting cousins). Sometimes, random forces intervene in your computing life. Animals and small people can amuse themselves by playing with your PC, leaving it in an unusual state. Cables can be unplugged, re-plugged, or borrowed for some other use. Software can be installed without a by-your-leave. DOG problems all fall into one of the other three categories as well, but they are unique in that you may be assuming that nothing on your PC has changed when it actually has.

The key to solving DOG problems is keeping track of what's been happening around your PC and securing it properly so all and sundry are not able to install software and change things without your knowledge.

Hardware

If none of the above situations apply, or if your PC or attached hardware feels or smells very hot, or the normal lights don't come on, or the screen doesn't display anything when you switch it on, you may have a hardware problem. We're not going to suggest ways to fix real hardware problems inside your PC, except to disconnect it from the mains power and talk to someone who's used to fixing such problems. We assume you don't want to tear the cover off the case and start poking about inside. If you do want to do that, we suggest you need to understand electrical safety first, and the correct handling of components sensitive to electrostatic discharge, not to mention the small print in your warranty.

If the hardware problem is to do with something you can unplug and still have a working PC – things like printers, scanners and modems – then just turn the PC off and unplug the hardware. You may need a new piece of hardware, but try updating the drivers before you get your wallet out. Restart your PC and continue with what still works.

If you can't tell a software problem from a hardware problem, maybe some diagnostic software can help. This can exercise your PC and report when it discovers an error.

The key to solving hardware problems is excluding software, user and DOG problems first. Once you know it's really hardware, seek help from someone qualified to fix it, or replace the hardware component if you can.

A REAL LIFE EXAMPLE

Not too long ago, one of our computers stopped producing any sound. Our first thought was that it was a DOG problem and that a kid had muted the sound without our knowing, but after checking it turned out that all the settings on the PC were OK. Next we checked for software problems, but all the drivers were up to date and everything seemed OK on that front. So we checked out all the hardware, and eventually discovered that the sound card in the PC had just died. The problem was fixed with a new sound card, but after that we discovered it had actually been a dog problem – literally. The dog had been sleeping under the desk on top of all the wires and rolled over on the on/off switch on the plug. The sudden loss of power had shorted out the sound card. The kid using the computer at the time had not bothered to tell us about this and the accompanying zapping sound from inside the PC box. Had they done so, it would have made diagnosing the problem a lot easier. In any case, now you know how DOG problems got their name.

Section 3:
Types of problems II

If nothing simple has worked, you've excluded DOG problems, checked all your cables and power leads, it's worth thinking about the problem in more detail. The better you can categorise the symptoms of your problem, the easier it'll be to match it against problems other people have had, and maybe find a solution.

When we talk about 'application programs' or 'applications' from now on, we mean all the stuff you use like browsers, email, word processors, games, media players and anything else that makes your PC useful to you – basically everything except Windows itself and bits of software like device drivers that you rarely even see unless they go wrong. You typically get these going from the Start menu or an icon or toolbar on the Desktop.

Now is a good time to get a notebook and start making notes about what you find on your PC, because things can get increasingly complicated from here.

It doesn't work at all

- If the 'it' that isn't working means not being able to boot your PC at all, you've got a hardware or a serious software problem. Do your best to exclude DOG problems by checking cables and hardware. Try starting Windows in Safe Mode (see Section 4 of Chapter One) and if that works you can then do a System Restore. If System Restore lets you boot your PC again normally, congratulations, you've fixed the problem. Try to remember what you did after the Restore Point you went back to and avoid doing it again in future. If the problem seems to have been caused by installing new hardware or software, or by using a particular function of an application, visit the manufacturer's website support section and see if they know about the problem. They might have a fix for the problem already.

- If Safe Mode doesn't help you boot, try using a bootable CD (see Section 4 of Chapter One).

- If Safe Mode and bootable CDs have both failed, you almost certainly have a hardware problem. Unless you really want to get into the nitty-gritty of your PC, which is beyond the scope of this book, now is the time to find a techie who may be able to help you. If you're lucky you'll have a friend who knows a lot about PCs and doesn't mind being asked to help for the umpteenth time. Local PC specialist stores often have knowledgeable people who may be able to set you right with just a quick chat. Large national chain stores often have service departments where they'll take your PC in and see if they can figure out what's wrong. (Remember what we said in Security.)

- If the 'it' that isn't working is an application, and it used to run but doesn't now, think about the valuable data you may have produced with it. Now is a good time to back up the data in addition to your regular backups. Then if things get much worse later, at least you've got the stuff you want. Now see What's Changed? (see Section 4 of this Chapter).

- If the 'it' that isn't working is an application you've never run before, you might need some other programs to help it run, or maybe it didn't install correctly, or maybe it'll never run at all. It can be worthwhile with a new application that doesn't work first time to simply uninstall it and reinstall it. This time round check for error messages or odd things during the installation process itself. Checking the manufacturer's website support section or forums will often turn up a solution for a problem like this: if something doesn't work first time, other people will usually have encountered the problem.

Some of it works, some of it doesn't

If your PC is partially working, we assume you can boot your machine up and start your application programs, but that something in an application is failing.

Did it ever work? If it did, see 'What's Changed?' in the next section as this is likely to be a user problem. Maybe you need to set some properties or preferences up in the program to make it work. Try the application's Help.

Another possibility is that some of your data has been corrupted. Now is another good time to back up the data associated with the program. Then if you're feeling adventurous, you could restore the data from an earlier backup and see if the problem goes away. If it does, then almost certainly something has corrupted your data – perhaps the application itself, or something you did recently, or maybe just a problem with hardware like a disk drive. Any time you begin to suspect a problem with your disk drive, you should immediately back up everything, just in case.

If restoring old data didn't change anything, you can then restore the data you backed up at the start of the previous paragraph, and you're back to where you were. It may not be working, but at least you've eliminated one possible fault.

Otherwise, maybe the new program is just broken. Lots of software is. You can usually find out by searching the Internet, because other disappointed users will probably have said so, probably at great length and with much bitterness. Maybe it'll be fixed in the next release, or has been fixed in a newer release. Maybe it won't, but at least then you can decide if you want to ditch the application completely and search for alternatives. If it's free software, there's not a whole lot you can do about it, but if you paid good money you can get a refund, or complain until the manufacturer fixes the problem. After all, dissatisfied customers are not good for business.

It works fine, but not all the time

Can you reproduce the problem? This is one of the most important things you can try and do. If a specific set of actions in a specific order (for example, opening a particular file) always causes the same problem, then when you're searching for reports of similar experiences you'll be able to zero in on the ones you want. When asking on a forum for help you can describe what's going on in enough detail for someone to perhaps recreate. If you can get to the point where someone else can create the same problem on their PC, then the chances of them being able to solve the problem are increased a hundredfold.

Absolutely the worst problems are those that appear randomly or only intermittently, and that cannot be recreated. If one application randomly experiences a problem, it's probably that application. But consider whether that's the only application to access a particular piece of hardware or file.

If the whole machine randomly reboots or replaces the whole Desktop with an error screen (the 'Blue Screen of Death' or BSOD) you probably have a hardware driver or actual hardware problem. Unplug as much hardware as you can except the PC screen and keyboard and see if it goes away.

If it doesn't, you may have an overheating problem and need help with your hardware. This is a common problem as PCs age and one of the hardest to nail down because it looks like the error may be down to a different program each time.

A REAL LIFE EXAMPLE

One of our PCs kept seizing up with no discernible pattern. It seemed a bit like an overheating problem, but only seemed to happen on cold days. It took a while to realise that it was indeed an overheating problem in the PC – on hot days, the desk fan was turned on, which cooled the PC enough to prevent the problem.

If the problem does go away, add back the hardware items you unplugged one at a time. See if you can find a combination that causes the problem to reoccur. If so, try updating the hardware drivers for those pieces of hardware. New drivers can be found on the manufacturer's website, and any time you suspect a problem with hardware it's always a good idea to update to the latest version of the drivers. It's unlikely to make things worse and it might do a great deal of good. If new drivers don't work, you may have

to stop using some of the hardware if you want a reliable
PC until you can find a solution, or get new hardware.

If the whole machine randomly locks up and pressing
Ctrl+Alt+Del won't display Task Manager (see Fig. 1)
you probably want to try reinstalling Microsoft Windows.
Make sure your backups are up to date before you do. If
reinstalling Windows doesn't improve the situation, you
probably have a hardware problem.

It looks like it's working, but it's producing garbage

You're doing what you think should work, but you're
not getting the results you want. Make sure you
understand what you're really trying to do and how to
do it in the application concerned. Given the state of the
documentation that comes with programs this isn't always
straightforward, but it's worth reading the application's
Help files. Posting a question to an online forum is also a
very good way to check if what you're doing should work
in the first place.

There's an old saying in the business – GIGO, or
'Garbage In, Garbage Out'. Computers are remarkably
good at doing exactly what they're told, no matter how
stupid that may be. You want every file on your computer
replaced by a photo of a goldfish? Sure, no problem. You
may well be unwittingly asking your application to produce
that garbage.

Check you're using the right version of the program for
any hardware or software it has to talk to. Most software has
a list of software and hardware requirements on the package,

in the manual, or in a ReadMe file in its installation folder. If it says it requires a USB 2.0 interface and all you've got is USB 1, there's your problem right there.

Your application program may be misconfigured or broken. If this is the case, you will need to search for similar reports on the Internet and see what other people did to fix or get round the problem.

It works, but at a glacial pace

Things running slowly is a common complaint. The first thing to check is what else is running on your PC.

A REAL LIFE EXAMPLE

One of our children complained constantly about his PC being slower than a snail, and when we did a quick check, he had about 25 programs running which had crept into the system by him installing things off the Internet willy-nilly. A quick session of deleting lots of unwanted programs through the Control Panel and the PC ran like a dream.

Display the **Task Manager** by pressing **Ctrl+Alt+Del**, or right-clicking on the **Taskbar** at the bottom of the screen and selecting **Task Manager** (see Fig. 1) and select the **Performance** tab (see Fig. 2).

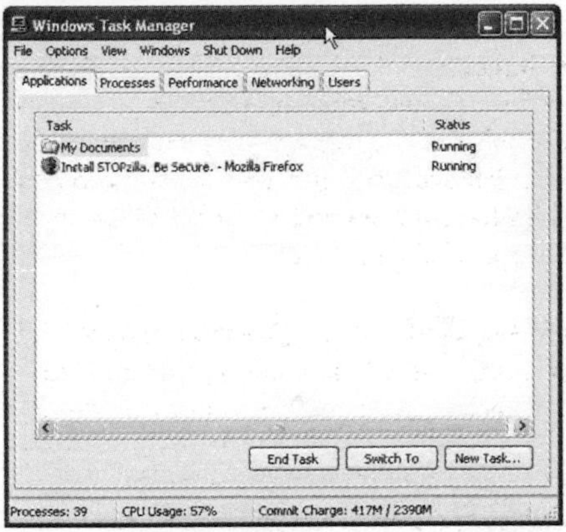

Figuring Out Where the Problem Is

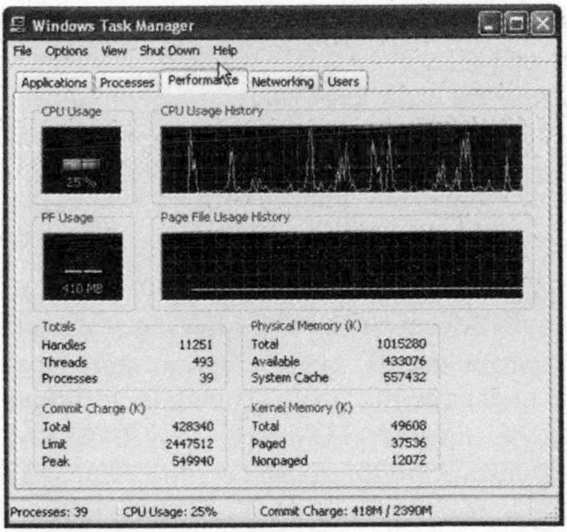

Fig. 1

Fig. 2

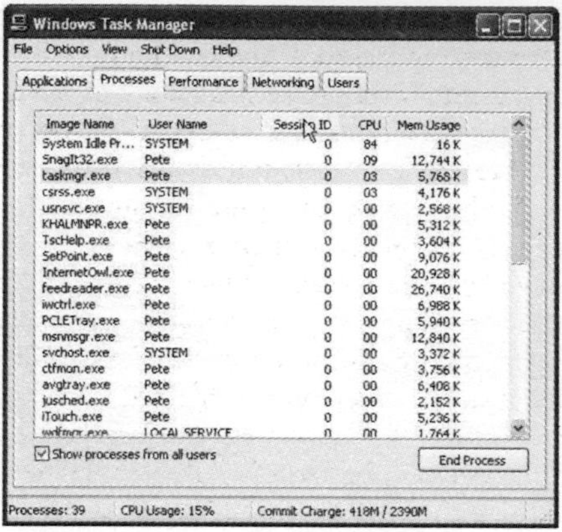

Fig. 3

Are the CPU Usage or memory graphs maxed out? If so, select the **Processes** tab and click on the column headings to order all the processes by memory or CPU use (see Fig. 3). The problem may not be in the application you're trying to use at all. Finding out what all those processes your PC runs are can be a challenge, but often their names are self-explanatory, and a quick search on Google with the name of the process or program may tell you a lot. If you can identify a process that's hogging the system, and it obviously relates to a specific application (for example: winword.exe is Word for Windows), you can try selecting that process and then clicking the End Process button. If your PC springs back into action, then you've identified the culprit. But be warned: terminating a process will probably lose any changes to data you've made while it's been running, and terminating a process you can't identify may well cause severe problems elsewhere.

When your anti-virus program is scanning your disk you may see a real slowdown in all your other programs. It's a good idea to schedule virus scans for times when you're not likely to be actively using the computer, like in the evening, early morning, or your lunch break.

Or maybe you've opened a huge document or image somewhere, or are doing something which uses a lot of the computer's processing power, like converting a film from your digital video camera to another format. The newer the software, the faster the processor or larger the memory it's likely to require. Check on the software's requirements – if it says you need 1 MB of RAM (memory) and you've only got half a MB on your PC, the program is spending its whole time reading, saving and reading data from the disk, and then finding out it needs to get rid of what it just saved and closed to make room for the data it read. If your PC doesn't meet the software's requirements there's not much you can do aside from not use the application in question. You could use an alternative application, get a new PC or, for the brave, install new memory or a new processor inside your PC.

If an application runs slowly when it's the first thing you start after booting your computer, maybe it'll never run fast on your machine, or maybe the machine is still doing the 1001 things it has to when it starts up and you just need to be patient and wait till it's ready to do real work. Wait until the hard drive light has stopped flashing when you restart your PC (long after the Desktop has appeared) before you do any performance testing. Otherwise, you need to identify the circumstances under which the slowdown occurs.

EXPERT TIP

If the **Task Manager** doesn't come up right away (and it may not because your PC is running so slowly), be patient and don't press *Ctrl+Alt+Del* again straight away – this is often a signal to the computer to reboot itself.

Section 4:
Looking for the problem

What's changed?

This question is often the key, but it is often also difficult to answer. If there are several people using your PC it can be nigh on impossible. This will be one of the first questions anyone trying to solve your problem will ask you, so try as hard as you can to identify and note down any changes you remember making. Sometimes problems don't become apparent until you've rebooted your PC, which can make life difficult. Sometimes you may not remember changing anything, but it could have been something as simple as a preference setting in an application, even a different application, which is the root of the problem. We can assure you that having worked in technical support for many years, the first thing you think of when someone tells you nothing has changed on their machine is 'Oh yeah, pull the other one' – one of the skills of technical support is learning not to say these things out loud.

If you can remember changing something, try to undo it and see if that helps. Set the options or preferences back where they were, or uninstall the application or hardware.

SOFTWARE ROT

As you use your PC, you often come across new applications you find useful or fun. Over a period of time, PCs usually accumulate a variety of useful or less useful add-ons, be they hardware or software. As this process continues, the sum of the changes can sometimes be much more than the sum of the parts as the different applications and hardware drivers can interfere with each other. The situation gets better with each release of Microsoft Windows, but we still often see the situation of software rot, where a PC has had so much installed on it that nothing really works properly any more. The less you add things to your PC the more stable it's likely to be. The only way out of a serious case of software rot may be to reinstall Microsoft Windows.

In fact, you might want to consider doing that every couple of years anyway. By starting afresh with a new installation of Windows and only the applications you actually use, you can get rid of a lot of stuff that's just hanging around doing nothing, but using time and effort to do that nothing. If you have a spare weekend, and a good set of backups, you can often give an old PC a new lease of life.

Wrestling with error messages

Your operating system and applications will sometimes display error messages. These can vary between the blindingly obvious to the completely obscure, such as: 'unhandled exception in thingamajig.exe reading petesdb at location x'007CDA439', Code 4063, rc=16'.

Whether they make sense or not, they're often a very useful clue as to what's going on. If you see error messages or error dialog boxes, make a note of them as accurately and completely as you can. Often you can simply select the message, cut and paste it into a text file and save it. We've seen lots of people asking for help describing incomplete or inaccurate error messages and this always makes it harder to identify the problem.

The contents of error messages are a very powerful tool for identifying your problem by searching the Internet. Try just typing the whole message into Google with quotation marks around it and see what you get. Double quotation marks tell Google to look for that exact sequence of words, not just pages where all of the words appear in any old order. If you get nothing, try picking the important words out of the error message, removing the quotation marks and searching for those. In the above example, 'Unhandled Exception', 'thingamajig.exe' and 'Code 4063' are all probably important to identify the problem, whereas 'petesdb' is obviously something to do specifically with the PC (which happens to be called PetesDesktop), and the location is something that may vary depending on the exact version of the application. The 'rc=16' may or may not be important, but you can always try searching with it and then without it if it didn't seem to help.

EXPERT TIP

If you're posting a question to a forum hoping someone else can help you sort the problem out, post the full error message, no matter how long, arcane and pointless it may seem. The more information other people have, the more likely they are to pinpoint something.

Checking audit trails

Audit files (or logs) are records of what a program is doing and any errors it may encounter doing this. Different applications write different amounts of useful information and pointless junk to these files, depending on the programmer who developed the application. Some applications may not have any audit files at all. The purpose of these files is to help programmers solve problems – even if most of what is in an audit file looks like Greek to you (or actually is Greek), you may be able to pick out valuable clues. Things like 'file not found' are usually excellent pointers to where the problem lies.

Ransack any Help files and other documentation you may have to find out whether your application writes audit files, and where. Usually it will be somewhere in the folders the application was installed into, but not always (and almost never on Linux systems). Look for files which are plain text (file extension '.txt') and called something like 'log'. A file called 'log.txt' is almost certain to be the one you're looking for. Try opening it in Notepad or WordPad. The most recent messages will be at the end, so just skip there and have a look. You might be surprised when the problem and potential solution just jump right out at you.

Some applications will write messages visible in the Microsoft Windows Event Viewer, which you can find in **Start-> Control Panel-> Administrative Tools-> Computer Management** (see Fig. 4 or Fig. 5 for Vista). This shows you various types of log. Examine them all, looking for entries marked in red.

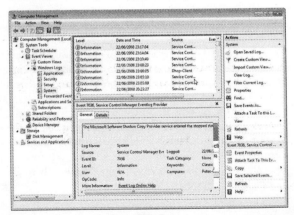

Fig. 4

Fig. 5

Gathering diagnosis information

That sounds pretty technical, doesn't it? But it's just what we've shown you how to do above. Log files, error messages, recent changes, problem symptoms, occurrences and so on are just the PC equivalents of medical case histories and disease symptoms that doctors use to diagnose what's wrong with a patient. In your case the PC is a patient, and you're the doctor (or at least a well-educated nurse or first-aider). Try to gather everything you can say about your problem in one place so you can review it.

You've asked yourself all the questions we list above and noted down the answers. Now try to reorganise your notes so you can understand them easily. If the easy pointers we mentioned above haven't fixed your problem, you need to go looking for the solution elsewhere.

Before you do that, you need to gather some other information that will make it easier to distinguish your PC problem from the many millions of other PC problems that exist.

- Which version of Microsoft Windows are you running exactly? Look in **Control Panel->System** (see Fig. 6 or Fig. 7 for Vista)

- Which version of your application are you running? Look in **Help->About**

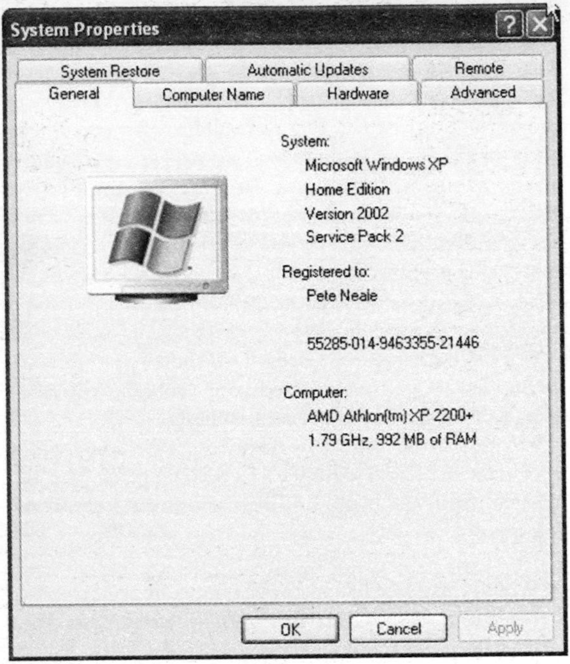
System Properties
System Restore
Automatic Updates
Remote
General
Computer Name
Hardware
Advanced
System:
Microsoft Windows XP
Home Edition
Version 2002
Service Pack 2
Registered to:
Pete Neale
55285-014-9463355-21446
Computer:
AMD Athlon(tm) XP 2200+
1.79 GHz, 992 MB of RAM
OK
Cancel
Apply

Fig. 6

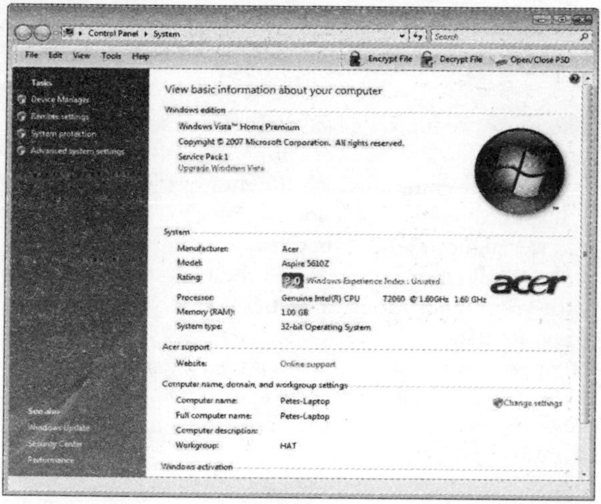

Fig. 7

When you're describing your problem to other people, or checking their description against yours, these are vital things to know. There's no point chasing down a problem and solution, only to find that you're dealing with a problem that was (supposedly) fixed in an older version of the application than you're using. It may be the same problem resurfacing, which is good to find out, but it's unlikely that whatever solution was found for the older version of the application will work on yours.

Section 5:
Looking for the solution

The most productive place to look for solutions is the Internet. It can also be a very unproductive place if you're just slavishly going through the motions.

If your computer won't boot, or can't access the Internet, you're caught in a bind, because you can't get online to look for solutions, or even read the Help files that came with your applications. The best thing is to have two computers and only break one at a time. Naturally, that's often easier said than done, but it's very hard to substitute for having the dead computer right next to a working one once you're convinced you haven't got a hardware error. Software is complicated.

Some possibilities include keeping an old Desktop PC or laptop around for emergencies (test it sometimes), using a friend or neighbour's PC, or using a library or Internet cafe. All of these are more or less difficult. Stealing your child's PC works well, for you anyway, if not for them. Making notes of your problem's diagnosis information is one thing, but trying to write the Internet on a piece of paper is quite another, and one that rarely goes well in our experience. ('I think we're going to need a bigger piece of paper…')

If you really can't tell the difference between a hardware and a software problem, so you still don't know what solution to look for, and you have no useful access to the Internet, your choices are limited. You should have some way of reinstalling Microsoft Windows, usually a CD, sometimes a recovery partition. Remember, you may lose your valuable data when you follow this option, but if a reinstall of Microsoft Windows fixes the problem, it wasn't hardware. It's a solution, but it's not an ideal one, because you have to laboriously rebuild your computer back to where it was before it went wrong. If you can do anything else before doing that, it's worth a try.

Google it

What techies love to do is document their successes and failures on the Internet. That can be punishingly boring as literature, but a lifeline when you have a problem.

The popular weblog or blog phenomenon has led to thousands of technical people who document their adventures with their computers. So there is a huge amount of information out there by people who have experienced the same problem as you. Even if they failed to solve the problem, it can be good to know that it's not just you and your PC that's going wrong.

Stare at your diagnosis information notes, and pick out the proper names and unusual words. Putting these words into Google or any other search engine of your choice will lead you to a world of blogs, emails and forums about all manner of technical matters.

There's no point in ploughing through thousands of Google pages reading the same stuff over and over. If you've scanned twenty or so pages and not seen anything relevant, try changing the Google search words – it will probably be much more productive. Don't seize on the first thing that sounds like your problem and try whatever it suggests. Consider the source from which you're reading. If it's got a date on it, think about whether it's recent or not. Recent is usually better, but if you've got an old PC or software, recent might not exist for you.

Blogs can be hard to understand or incomplete. They often contain links and other clues to where to go to find further information. If the page you're viewing doesn't make some sort of sense reasonably quickly, just move on. There's always another 478,613 page hits to consider, and at least one should make sense.

The best source of information about your problem is often the mailing lists and forums that exist for most major application programs. These are often populated by knowledgeable and helpful people who love to answer questions.

Seriously, it's true. Techies love to help out other people, partly because they like to show off and feel important, but mostly because they really do understand that the more they help other people, the more others will help them (or someone else).

Anyway, if you can find several people talking about your problem, you know you've identified it well. If you find your problem being asked about, but no one ever replies, it may be what the techies think is a question too obvious to answer. Look again at any Help documents you can find for the application.

On the other hand, if you find only a couple of exact descriptions of your problem, with some other poor souls pleading for help in fixing it but no one has replied to them, this is good. Not 'good' that no one has replied (though the odds are good that someone who knows how to fix the problem hasn't seen their plea), but 'good' that someone else has the exact same problem. It makes it that much more likely that you'll find a solution somewhere, so keep looking. Maybe even take a few good keywords from their problem description and add them to your Google search.

Ask in a forum

Your search engine results have led you to the forums and email lists where people talk about your application, or things that look like your problem. Nothing you've read quite matches your exact experience, though. You can ask. Don't be afraid, that's exactly what the forums are there for (though you may have to register first). And the good thing is that if you do end up asking something that turns out to be an incredibly stupid question with an appallingly obvious answer, at least they don't know who you are so you can get away without feeling embarrassed.

You've asked your question, now will some technical angel answer? Three possibilities arise.

● The first is no replies at all, even after a couple of days. If there seems to be recent traffic on the forum, you may have asked a question the denizens consider too obvious to even answer. Think about whether you're in the right forum – if there's a choice between a 'developer' and a 'user' forum, you probably want the 'user' one. You can try posting a plaintive follow-up saying you're a complete newbie, and can someone at least tell you where to ask for help, please?

● The second possibility is an unhelpful or even insulting reply. If you want to get to the bottom of your PC problem, you'd best not reply in the same way or you may be drawn into a 'flame war', where people online exchange colourful insults. These tend to be a waste of everyone's time. See if there's anything positive you can possibly get out of an unhelpful reply. Maybe someone is trying to give you a clue about where you could look to find out what you need to know. And if you're polite and positive despite someone calling you names, it's likely that some kind soul will jump in and try to steer you in the right direction.

● The third and best possibility is you find someone who knows what your problem is likely to be and is prepared to describe how you might deal with it. If the forum is run by the manufacturer of the software your chances of this may be higher than when you're in a public forum supported by advertising, but you may have to pay for access to the manufacturer's forum.

Once you've had the experience of finding someone to guide you through fixing your problem you'll start to realise the true collaborative power of the Internet. Your description of the problem and its resolution are now available for anyone else to read, helping everyone to better understand their PC.

EXPERT TIP

Try to make your question as short and polite as you can, while describing your problem as well as you can. You may be feeling highly frustrated, but it's not usually relevant to getting your question answered.

Telephone helplines

Telephone helplines can be expensive and frustrating, so try remembering things could be worse – you could be the poor so-and-so on the other end.

Helplines can be very bad at tracking your problems – each time you phone it's as if you've never called before. The chances of getting the same person on the end twice are almost zero. Queues are long and, if it's a particularly knotty problem, you may have to fight your way through layers of personnel until you get someone who actually understands the product at a fundamental level – if that's even possible. You might seriously consider cutting your losses and trying a different approach.

Most hardware and software manufacturers don't provide telephone support at a price a home user is prepared to pay. All the same, it's best to check any manufacturer's documentation for information on extra support services. Check the manufacturer's website as it may have a live chat facility, which is sometimes better than a telephone helpline (and sometimes worse), or email support, which is usually better as you tend to get a slightly more knowledgeable person on the other end.

The person you speak to on a helpline is likely to be non-technical and working from a script with a strictly limited number of options. These are almost invariably biased towards reinstalling things to find out whether there's a hardware problem. Even if you can clearly and concisely describe exactly what the problem is, a person working from a script is unable to do anything with this information. You have to wade through the script with them, convince them you've tried all the solutions like reinstalling and rebooting that they've suggested and wait for them to pass the problem on to someone further down the chain. If the helpline operator suggests you reinstall Microsoft Windows, you need to think about whether your valuable data is backed up first.

That said, following such scripts can be useful if you're still not sure whether you have a hardware problem or not.

If all this sounds a bit negative, well, it is, but it's not entirely the fault of the helpline. They get masses of calls, and more often than not it's a really stupid problem and easily solved by working through a set of standard questions and suggestions. It goes without saying this doesn't apply to your problem, but it would be far too expensive to employ technical experts to answer all those phones, especially if most solutions don't require much technical knowledge. The system is not pleasant for anyone involved, but it does make supporting programs used by millions of people possible.

On rare occasions, you find a helpline with good problem tracking and people who are able to help you. If this happens, make a mental note to use them again and let them know they've done a great job.

Chapter 3:
Hardware Problems

We're not going to go into too much detail about how to fix
hardware problems, because this often requires extensive
spare hardware resources. Without exotic test equipment,
the only way to decide whether a given piece of hardware
works or not is to swap it with another one and see what
changes. If you're going to go down this route, it's best to
clearly label the parts you're swapping, and keep careful
notes of what you do.

Of course, if you have another PC on which you can
try things out, this can often be useful. Things that plug
into your PC can easily be swapped, and you can decide
whether it's the PC itself or the plugged hardware that's
at fault.

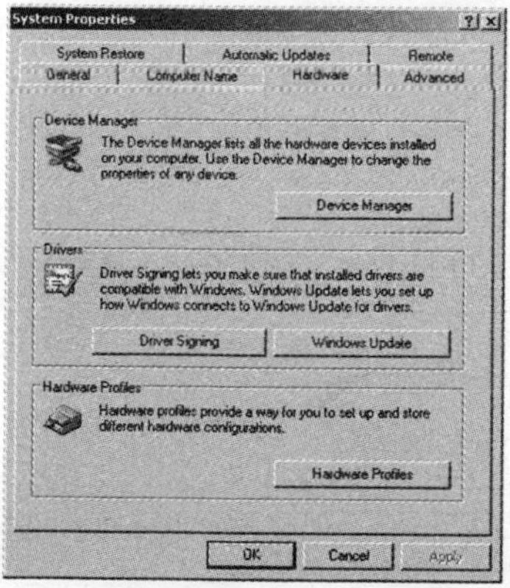

Fig. 1

Fig. 2

Fig. 3

DEVICE MANAGER

Assuming your PC gets as far as starting Microsoft Windows, you can find out a lot about your system's hardware by looking in **Device Manager**. Go to **Start**, **Control Panel** and select **System** (see Fig. 1). In the **System Properties** dialog box, select the **Hardware** tab. Click the **Device Manager** button (see Fig. 2).

You can now see an expanding list (or tree) view of your hardware arranged by category. When everything in a category is working fine, it's closed by default. When there's a problem, the tree is opened up to show you the device. In Fig. 3, Device Manager is showing that there is a problem with PCI Modem. A device with a yellow question mark means Microsoft Windows has found some hardware, but it doesn't have a hardware driver for it. A red X means the device is damaged somehow. Right-click on the device and select Properties to learn more about what seems to be wrong.

If you think you should have a piece of hardware available and it doesn't show up in Device Manager then the computer isn't seeing the attached device at all. You probably have a cable problem or a hardware problem on that device.

EXPERT TIP

Almost every hardware problem may be down to a cable problem. Whatever the problem is, it's usually worthwhile checking the cables and plugs as a first step.

Section 1:
Basic PC components

Connections (cables and plugs)

Loose connections are a frequent source of PC headaches. Cables get pulled, pushed, trodden on and snagged on other things. Even when left alone, over time marginal connections can fail. Connection problems usually cause dramatic symptoms: something won't work at all. You might even see error messages of some sort.

Action 1

Check cables for any signs of damage. If it's a damaged power cable, you are looking at a serious hazard. Turn off the power at the mains outlet, unplug the cable and don't try to use the device it's connected to until the cable is replaced. Discard the damaged cable.

Action 2

If you suspect a connection problem, power off your PC and remove and reconnect each plug firmly, even if you're sure it was connected in the first place. Then power the PC back on and see if the device is now working.

USB ports

Most PCs have two or more USB (Universal Serial Bus) ports – rectangular sockets about half an inch on their long edge. In principle, you can plug any USB device into a USB port and Microsoft Windows will recognise it and make it available for your use.

As usual with computers, a great-sounding idea is actually a little more complicated than it first appears. To begin with, there have been at least two generations of USB ports. (The second generation is known as USB 2.0 but, like world wars, they hadn't thought of numbering them when the first generation came out so it's often just called USB.) Naturally, the later ones are faster than the earlier ones (much like the difference between blitzkrieg and trench warfare). Plugging an earlier device into a later port usually works well. Plugging a later device into an earlier port on your PC can fail to work altogether, or only work very slowly.

Looking in Device Manager in the Universal Serial Bus Controllers tree will let you know whether you have any USB controllers and what kinds. There is often a mixture of generations on one computer. It can be hard to match the USB sockets on your PC to the controllers inside, so if a USB device seems unresponsive or slow, try it in some other USB sockets to see if things get better.

USB devices can draw their power from the cable attached to your PC. While this can work well, some PCs, especially laptops, have severely limited power supply capacity. If a USB device can get its power from either the mains or the USB port itself, it's usually a good idea to plug the mains in. With laptops, you may find USB devices that won't work until both the device and the laptop are on mains power.

You can expand the number of USB devices attached by using a USB hub. This is a small box with a USB cable that plugs into one socket on your PC, and in turn provides several sockets for USB devices to plug into. If you have a limited number of USB ports on your PC, or you want to simplify your cabling, a USB hub can be convenient. Difficulties can arise when USB devices plugged into the hub interfere with each other, or draw too much power for the hub. Strange and intermittent problems can result. A mixture of different generation USB devices on a hub can cause slowdowns or failures.

When you experience problems involving USB devices, it's always a good idea to:

- Use the shortest USB cable you can, definitely shorter than two metres (six feet)

- Use mains power everywhere you can

- Plug the device directly into a USB port on your PC, with no external hub

Having coaxed the device into operation, you can try using an external hub and, if that works, sharing the hub with other devices. If plugging an additional device into the hub causes some or all of the other devices to stop working then that's probably too much for the hub and you'll have to find another USB port for the new device.

Self-powered hubs (with their own power supply) are often more reliable than those that depend on your PC's USB power. More recent PCs will probably have enough USB ports to make an external hub unnecessary, although laptops can still be sorely lacking.

PC

The boxy thing everything else plugs into is technically called the system unit. We'll just call it the PC as that's what everyone else calls it. It contains the processor, the memory, and the hard disk that provides long-term storage of your operating system, applications and data. If the PC is not working, nothing else is going to work, so if you have an 'it doesn't work at all' problem before you've even seen a Microsoft Windows Desktop you should start here. If you can see the Windows Desktop or sign on screen, you have a problem elsewhere.

When you press the power switch on your PC, you expect the light on the front to come on and to hear the fan or fans running. If that doesn't happen, you probably have a power cable problem (see Connections) or a PC hardware problem.

Action 1

Check the power cable is firmly attached and the wall power outlet is working. If the wall power outlet appears at all broken, do not use it. Call a qualified electrician immediately.

Action 2

If you have a spare power cable, try swapping it in. If the PC now has power, it's worth checking the fuse in the plug, or just throw away the old power cable.

Action 3

Check whether the PC has a power on/off switch at the back which has become switched to off. If you still don't see the power light, and you still don't hear the fans, you need hardware help. If you can hear the fans but the light isn't on, then it may be just the little light that's damaged. If the rest of the PC is working now, you can ignore the lack of light.

So, we now assume the power light is on and the fans are running.

When you turn the power on, the BIOS program of your PC wakes up and tries to check the hardware. One beep from the PC speaker is a good sign – the BIOS check has passed. If you hear more than one beep from the PC speaker when you have a keyboard plugged in, this usually indicates the BIOS has found a hardware problem.

Action 1

Check the keyboard (as this is one of the first pieces of hardware the BIOS checks) and try again. The lights on the keyboard should flash if the BIOS detects the keyboard. If they don't, there may be a hardware problem with the PC.

Action 2

If you hear nothing at all but the fans, don't worry, maybe the speaker's disconnected. Power off and connect a screen, ideally one with its own power cord to the wall, then power on again and see if anything at all appears on the screen. If you can see anything at all, congratulations, you're through to the BIOS. If you don't see anything, and the screen works on another PC, you have a hardware problem inside your PC and we suggest you seek help from a hardware expert.

If you've got this far, your PC is working to some extent. It's not useful to you yet. The next thing that should happen is Microsoft Windows starts up, with a nice big logo to let you know. If that doesn't happen, and you get a message that looks like 'unable to boot' on the screen, you need to check your disk drive.

Your PC contains at least one hard disk drive. That's the one Microsoft Windows is on, and it's the one that has to be working. The inside of a hard disk drive is a marvel of precision engineering, but consequently somewhat prone to failure. Physical shocks, especially while the drive is running, can easily lead to damage. Precision bearings within the drive wear out.

Action 3

If you've got as far as the PC BIOS, but Microsoft Windows does not appear, access the BIOS (see Section 4 of Chapter One). Here you'll be able to see whether the BIOS can talk to your hard drive, which should appear in a list of your internal hard drives and CD-type drives. It may be a bit hard to find your hard drive amongst all the BIOS screens. If it's not immediately obvious, try looking for IDE devices and channels. If there's no sign of your hard disk, you have a hardware problem inside your PC. If the hard drive seems to be there, you probably have a serious software problem and you will need to boot from a CD to recover.

Disk drives

We've mentioned your PC will have at least one hard disk drive. It's unusual to see more than one drive on normal PCs, so you probably only have one. Recent hard drives are of an enormous capacity and you might never need more space than comes in the box. On the other hand, your valuable data has a way of getting bigger all the time.

Still, it's often convenient to attach another hard drive for backup, or to share files. The most common way of doing that is by USB. What's supposed to happen is you plug the drive into any USB port, a small message bubble appears on your Desktop to inform you the disk was attached and the drive appears with its own drive letter in Microsoft Windows.

If that doesn't happen, it's most likely to be a cable problem. If cable changing (see Connections, earlier in the section) doesn't help, there are some other things you can try.

Action 1
Make sure you plug the hard drive USB cable directly into a USB port on the PC case, bypassing any USB external hubs. If the hard drive seems excessively slow, try another USB port.

Action 2
Still no joy? Try the external hard drive on another PC.

Action 3
If the drive doesn't work on a different PC as well, try swapping the USB cable for a different one.

Action 4
If that doesn't help, it's probably a broken external hard drive. If it's new, you could do worse than returning it

to the dealer and asking for a new one. If it's an old one, we hope you read the section on backing up and took it to heart.

Screen

After your PC and its disk drive, the screen is the most important component for fixing problems. If there's no working screen, your PC can only communicate with beeps. Unless you are C3P0 that's not going to be very helpful to you.

The screen cable sometimes requires a small screwdriver to properly attach to its plug; otherwise, there may be finger screws. Either way, make sure any cable screws are properly tightened.

Action 1

If your PC has beeped once after you turned it on and you see nothing at all on the screen, but its power light is on, the best thing is to try it on another PC. If it works there, your PC has a hardware problem. If it doesn't work on another PC, the screen has a hardware problem.

EXPERT TIP

Does your screen look fuzzy? Is one edge missing? Is it difficult to focus on? You should try to fix that. Prolonged work at a hard-to-read screen is bad for you.

If your screen displays things in odd colours, or mainly a single colour, you probably have a cable problem. Red, green and blue signals often travel down the cable on single wires and one or more of them aren't getting through.

First understand that screens display the images you see as a large number of dots. Each screen has a number of dots it's best at displaying, called its 'native resolution'. A common one is 1,024x768 – that's 1,024 dots (or pixels) per line, arranged in 768 horizontal lines – although better screens with more dots are constantly arriving on the market at cheaper prices. More dots let you display better-looking images, and a larger Desktop area. We always buy the largest screens we can afford, because we think a large screen area makes more difference to a computer's usefulness than almost anything else.

How do you find out a screen's native resolution? If you're lucky, you have a booklet to tell you; otherwise, look at what's written on the screen's casing, or the box it came in, and search on the Internet. Sometimes it's obvious you've found the native resolution, because the screen suddenly looks so good.

You can often tell the PC's graphics adaptor card, which drives the screen, to display more dots than the native resolution. The screen will do its best, up to a point, but will only be able to display lots of fuzzy dots, instead of fewer sharp ones. Conversely, you can tell the graphics adaptor to display fewer dots than the native resolution. This looks like a small Desktop, with big, blocky graphics on it.

Action 1

You set the graphics adaptor up in software by right-clicking on the Desktop and selecting **Properties** (see Fig. 4). (In Vista you click on **Personalize** – the screens and options which follow are laid out somewhat differently, but it should be fairly obvious.) A dialog box will open; select the **Settings** tab. Here you'll find controls that let you set up the resolution you'll see on the screen and sometimes the colour balance too. It's best to make adjustments carefully, in small steps, as some graphics adaptors can send signals to the screen you're using that it won't be able to display.

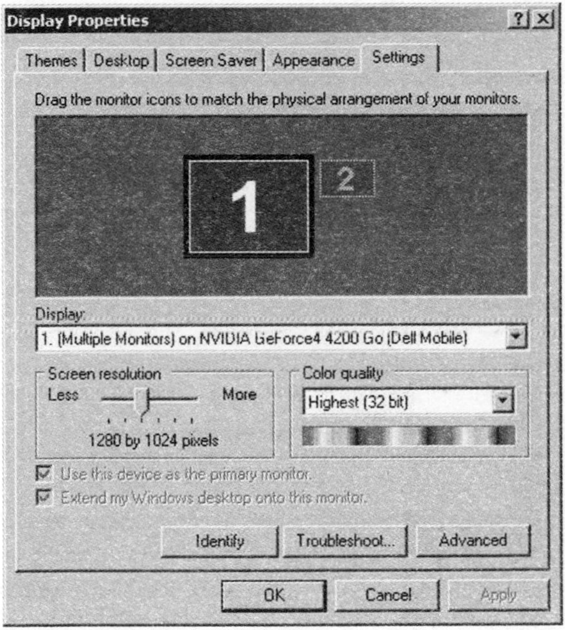

Fig. 4

EXPERT TIP

Many PC manufacturers automatically install more sophisticated applications for changing the display settings on your PC. If you have one of these, you may need to use it to change the settings instead of the default Windows Desktop properties. These vary widely depending on the manufacturer, but they should all be accessible by clicking on **Start** and then searching through **All Programs**, and they should all be documented in the manuals that came with your PC.

Action 2

If you increase your screen resolution and the screen goes blank, or displays a message like 'No Signal', wait a while and it should return to its previous resolution. Otherwise, you will see a dialog box asking you whether to continue at the new resolution. If you think it's the right one, press **Yes**.

So you've got your graphics adaptor set to your screen's native resolution, and you're still not happy with how it looks. Try the controls on the front of the screen itself. Often one of them (usually called auto-adjust) automatically matches the screen to the graphics adaptor. Otherwise, you might have to find that control in a menu system the screen will display for you. Adjusting the screen often makes a very positive difference. If you change the graphics card resolution again, always tell the screen to readjust itself for the changed resolution.

Keyboard

If no lights flash on your keyboard when you turn your computer on, and your keyboard doesn't work, it's almost certainly a cable problem (see Connections). Check carefully that the keyboard plug is in the right socket on the PC. If you have a wireless keyboard, you still need to check the cable from the wireless receiver to your PC, as well as replacing the batteries in the keyboard itself. But if your wireless keyboard isn't working, it's always useful to have an old spare wired keyboard you can try to make sure the problem is with the keyboard itself.

Usually, keyboards more or less work but they can be very annoying, with keys that stick and keys that don't work. Your keyboard may be hard to adjust so it's comfortable.

EXPERT TIP

With older PCs which use small round plugs for the keyboard and mouse (called PS/2 style connectors), a common contusion is plugging the mouse and keyboard connectors into each other's sockets on the PC. If both your mouse and your keyboard fail to work and they have these PS/2 connectors, check for them being in the wrong socket. If the sockets are colour coded, green is the mouse and violet is the keyboard. If they're not colour coded, there may be a tiny picture of a keyboard or a mouse next to each socket. Newer PCs will have USB keyboards and mice, which are supposed to work in any USB port.

If your keyboard is annoying you, we say replace it. You can prise the key caps off and hoover the crumbs out if you like, but any keyboard old enough to have accumulated enough crumbs to make a difference is probably old enough to need replacing anyway.

Action 1

Keyboards are notoriously prone to beverage spills. Ensure no liquid has got into the PC. If you think it has, power off immediately at the wall plug, and seek hardware help. Once you're sure it's just the keyboard, try to shut down normally, then unplug and replace the keyboard.

Action 2

You might be able to salvage the wet keyboard by washing it in clean, warm running water for several minutes, gently shaking as much water out as possible, then leaving it for at least 48 hours in a warm, dry place. Airing cupboards work well. Whatever you do, don't iron it. Try the washed and dried keyboard out, and if it works, keep it as a spare, as its long-term reliability is seriously compromised by this process.

EXPERT TIP

Always make sure your keyboard is at a comfortable height and distance from you when you use it. Badly-positioned keyboards can lead to cramp and repetitive strain injury. We like changing our posture regularly as we sit at the PC for long periods, so the keyboard needs to go with us.

Mouse

The mouse used to consist of a small box with a plastic ball at the bottom, rolling round on your desk. Movements of the ball were transmitted to the mouse pointer on your screen. An industry grew up making vanity mouse mats, because your desk wasn't well designed for the plastic balls available. Mouse mats got grubby and worn and the edges peeled away, and mouse mechanics wore and gummed up. PC owners struggled to move the mouse pointer round the screen.

Luckily, the twenty-first century has brought us optical mice, which shine light onto almost any surface to detect movement. No need for a mouse mat, and a much smoother experience. If you have a mouse with a mechanical ball on the bottom, we recommend you replace it. Even better are wireless mice, although you need to keep a supply of batteries to hand.

REAL LIFE EXAMPLE

One of us has an old-fashioned desk with a leather top, and optical mice don't work well on it at all. But ball mice work a treat, and the leather is better than any mouse mat.

Like your keyboard, your mouse has a profound effect on how easy it is to use your PC, and if it is not well positioned it can lead to cramp or repetitive strain injury. As well as being exposed to human touch, mice suffer from all the hazards like paper dust and coffee that abound on your desk.

Action 1

Once its cable is correctly plugged in, your mouse will usually work to some degree. If it doesn't, replace it, or replace batteries in wireless mice and try again. If the mouse seems difficult to use, stiff or sticky, replace it as soon as possible.

Action 2

If the mouse pointer on your screen seems to move too quickly or too slowly in response to mouse movements, go to the **Start Menu**, open **Control Panel** and click on the mouse icon. A dialog box will appear to let you make adjustments to your mouse pointer response (see Fig. 5). You may be able to set up any extra buttons and wheels on your mouse here too.

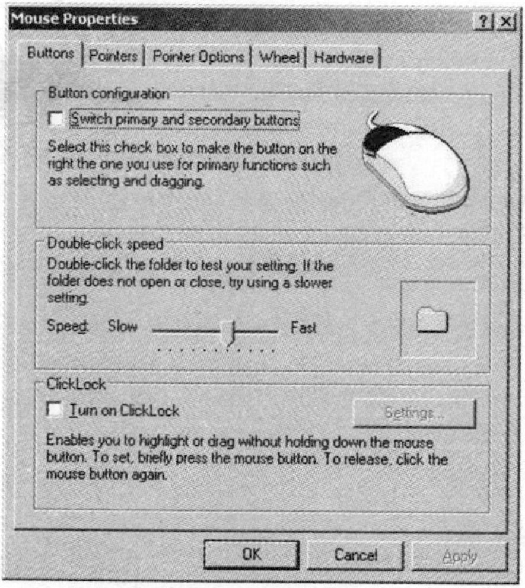

Fig. 5

Action 3

If adjustments seem to make no difference, examine the mouse for branding and product information and make sure the mouse dialog box corresponds to the actual mouse you're using. If it doesn't, you'll need to locate and install the correct drivers for your mouse.

Speakers

Speakers plug into your PC's sound card and usually have a power supply of their own. The most common initial speaker problems are cable problems: either the speaker power is not plugged in, or the speaker input is not connected to the sound card correctly.

Action 1

Sound cards usually have several colour-coded sockets, so there's plenty of room for error when plugging in the speakers. If you can't hear anything, try plugging the speakers into different sockets and see if anything happens.

Action 2

If your speakers stop working, make sure your Windows Desktop volume is turned up and not on mute. This is the most common speaker error, since other programs and relatives can helpfully mute your sound for you. By default, Windows usually displays a little speaker icon in the Taskbar which you can use to change the volume and/or mute the sound. If you can't see the speaker icon, go to the **Start** Menu, select **Control Panel** and click on **Sound and Audio** (see Fig. 6). As you adjust the volume slider,

Windows should play a bell tone for you. Make sure any **Mute** boxes are unticked.

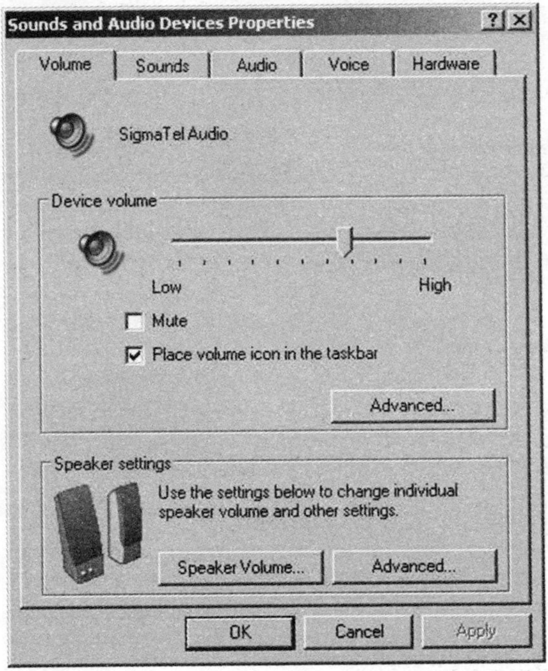

Fig. 6

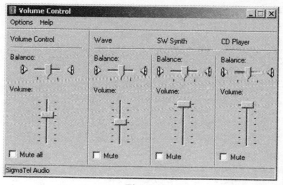

Fig. 7

Action 3

If your speakers work, but sound bad, try adjusting any volume control on the speaker and the Desktop volume control at the same time to see if you can make them sound any better. To access the Desktop Volume Control (Fig. 7) go to **Start-> Control Panel-> Sounds and Audio Devices-> Volume**. Turning one up and the other down can help, or vice versa. If your speakers sound rattly or buzzy, they're probably broken, or really cheap and nasty.

CDs and DVDs

CDs and DVDs are examples of optical drives. These take a thin, saucer-sized disk with a prismatic-looking surface on one side. A CD holds data equivalent to about 70 minutes of music, or about 650 MB. A DVD holds about five times that, nearly 5 GB, although special DVDs will hold twice as much by writing data on two layers of the disk. The latest generation of optical disks, Blu-Ray, holds about five times a standard DVD, at 25 GB. Manufacturers are promising to deliver Blu-Ray disks with four layers, offering a disk you can slip in your pocket with 100 GB of data on it.

Because of their unmatched ability to produce cheap, high-volume disks, optical media have become the method of choice for distributing computer software and data as well as entertainment, and provide outstandingly cost-effective data storage for PC users.

EXPERT TIP

Numbers in computers are usually measured these days in units of kilobytes (KB or K), megabytes (MB or M) and gigabytes (GB or G). These terms don't mean much to most people, although they can tell that 100 MB is obviously four times as big as 25 MB. They are simply shorthand terms, just as a kilogram is short for 1,000 grams.

The (almost) basic unit of information in a computer is a byte. For example, one character in a word document takes one byte to store (unless you're Japanese or Chinese, but we won't go into that). As a rough rule of thumb, 1 KB is a thousand bytes, 1 MB is a million bytes, and 1 GB is a thousand million bytes . Adding another set of three zeroes on the end gives you a terabyte (TB), or a million MB.

Don't confuse these terms with Kb and Mb (note the lower-case second letter), which refer to bits. A byte is made up of eight bits, but otherwise the prefixes retain the same meaning. So, if your broadband connection downloads 1 Mb per second, that's a million bits or 125,000 bytes (125K) – it will actually take eight seconds to download 1 MB of data.

With these various disks available, not all optical drives will be able to read and write all of them. The disks an optical drive knows about are usually indicated by small logos marked on the front of the drive itself. Device Manager is an excellent way to find out about your optical drive's capabilities. The device name will probably include the letters CD or DVD. If the drive can write optical disks, the name will include RW (read and write) after the CD or DVD. In any case, Device Manager usually tells you enough for an Internet search to reveal full details (see start of this chapter about accessing Device Manager).

Optical drives are often found in separate enclosures (small metal boxes), and you can attach them to your PC by a USB cable. The drive should immediately show up with a drive letter and be visible in Device Manager. Recent PCs may let you boot optical media off a USB-attached optical drive, though you may need to look at the BIOS to enable it.

Optical drives spin their media at extreme speeds, so whooshing and whirring sounds are normal, although the quieter a drive, the better. Rattling or clicking sounds are usually a bad sign.

Action 1

Sometimes it's possible to misalign the disk when putting it in the drive, so if you hear an odd sound and you can't read the disk, try ejecting it, pick the disk up and realign it, and try again.

When optical drives fail, they usually become unable to read disks other PCs have no problem with. Sometimes an RW drive loses the ability to read before it loses the ability to write. If your optical drive is showing signs of getting crotchety, it's best to seek hardware help and get it replaced.

Action 2

The prismatic side of an optical disk can be scratched or abraded quite easily, making it hard or impossible to read. You can try the disk in a couple of other PCs. If you're lucky, one of them may be able to read it. If it's a disk you can replace, the best thing is to replace it and dispose of the scratched one. If it's an irreplaceable disk, maybe a backup, you need to try to find a disk polishing kit in a computer shop. These can help, but it's not guaranteed. Better to treat optical disks with care; keep them in a case when they're not in the optical drive and always try and touch only the edges to avoid such problems.

If you're writing your backups on optical disks, we can't emphasise enough the importance of buying quality media for this purpose. 'No name' disks can cost half the price or less of name brand manufacturers', but there's a reason for that. Tests show that cheap disks often have hugely higher error rates than name brand media. Clever coding of the data means you can still read them, but for long-term backup storage cheap disks have no headroom to allow for inevitable age-related deterioration. Cheap disks are fine for passing big files around between computers, but for backup we recommend you choose quality at a price.

Optical media usually come in two forms, -R or –RW. The -R suffix can be written to just once, whereas the -RW type can be erased and written to again.

You may think CD-RW or DVD-RW disks are a good idea for backup, because you can use them again. We don't. Writeable backup media may be overwritten by accident just when you need them. One of the things we like best about write-once disks is once you've written them, they usually stay written for a long time. -RW disks are usually more physically fragile than -R disks when they're exposed to light and heat.

While the latest generation of optical media is usually quite expensive, the previous generation is usually very cheap. As we write, the most expensive CD-Rs are available for less than a pound, and it's possible to buy quality media for less than 50 pence. Soon DVD-R will be as just as cheap, if it isn't by the time you're reading this. It seems a small price to pay to ensure your valuable data can't be overwritten.

When you're using optical media for backup, it's often convenient to store the disks you write in a 'cake' container, rather than individual jewel cases. Store the container somewhere dark, cool and dry, like a desk drawer. We've seen people storing optical media on window sills – not recommended. If the plant watering doesn't get them, the sunlight will.

If you want to dispose of your backups, think carefully. They may contain sensitive data. To dispose of one disk, first wrap it in a plastic bag, then break it with your hands. The plastic bag is there to contain the sharp shards which might otherwise fly off. If you regularly dispose of optical media, we recommend you get a shredder designed to shred CDs as well as paper. Be careful how you empty the hopper, as lots of tiny pieces of static, sticky plastic are released in the shredding process.

Old CDs and DVDs also make dandy coasters for protecting your desk.

EXPERT TIP

Always read the label.

It may seem obvious, but clearly labelling your backup media, with contents and the date and time the backup was made, really can save you hours later on. 'Quick backups' when you're in a hurry, with a terse-to-non-existent label, are hard to interpret days later, when you want to extract a particular version of a file.

For optical media, it's best to use a marker pen specifically designed for the job.

Section 2:
Printers and scanners

Printer

Printing can be a huge source of frustration. In this hardware section, our aim is to get to the point where the printer connected to your PC can print a test page. Problems beyond this point are dealt with in the software and networking sections. We say 'the printer attached to your PC', because we're not talking about networked printers. If your printer plugs straight into a socket on your PC, it's not networked. If it plugs into a router or a hub or a different PC, or it's wireless, it is networked.

Industrial printers come at prices that suggest some paddocks and outbuildings might be part of the deal. Your Desktop printer does essentially the same job, moving sheets of paper around and printing text and graphics on them to within millimetre distances, for about 100,000th of the industrial price. Obviously, some compromises have to be made. Printer engineers have done an amazing job making Desktop printers both cheap and reliable, but once the paper handling clockwork in your printer goes wrong, there's little you can do to improve the situation. Usually, you can limp along for a while, hand feeding sheets or pressing the buttons on the front to encourage the printer to pick the next sheet up, but a printer that doesn't work reliably should be replaced as soon as possible.

The only replacement item on most Desktop printers is the ink or toner cartridge. Many printer manufacturers will sell you a printer at a cheap price, hoping to make the money back by selling you printer ink cartridges. These can be expensive, but think carefully before buying in bulk. Printer models come and go with surprising speed, and if your printer fails you may not be able to get another one that will accept your bulk-bought ink. When buying ink for an older printer, check whether it's cheaper to buy a new printer with ink. This seems perverse, but it sometimes happens.

EXPERT TIP

Some shops offer compatible printer cartridges at much cheaper prices, as well as sometimes refilling your old cartridge when it runs out. If you do a lot of printing, this could make quite a large financial difference for you, but be warned: if you do not use the manufacturer's own brand cartridges, it may well invalidate any guarantee on your printer.

Desktop printers use inkjet or laser technology to print. Laser printers are usually more expensive and also more reliable. If you do a lot of printing, laser printers can be more economical, especially if they can print on both sides of the paper.

Printers connect to your PC by parallel cables or USB cables. Sometimes, printers can be connected by either type of cable. Never connect both. USB is often easier to manage.

Action 1

If your USB printer doesn't seem to work, try to connect the USB cable directly to the PC, bypassing any USB hubs you have. Parallel cables should be connected before you turn your PC on. Either way, your printer should turn up in Device Manager. If it doesn't, you have a cable or a printer hardware problem.

Action 2

For USB printers, try a different USB port on your PC.

Action 3

If you can see your printer in Device Manager (see start of this chapter about accessing Device Manager), but there's a yellow question mark next to it, you need to install a driver for your printer. This is an increasingly rare occurrence as Microsoft Windows recognises most printers these days and will find suitable drivers for them on the Internet. As usual, a red X indicates a hardware problem.

Action 4

Open the **Start** menu and from the **Control Panel** select **Printers and Faxes**. Right-click your printer and select

Properties. On the **General** tab, press the **Print Test Page** button. If all is well, your printer will produce a legible test page.

Action 5

If nothing happens, double-click your printer's icon in the Printers and Faxes window. This should display the queue of print jobs and their status. If there's no queued job, your PC sent the job to the printer, so look at the printer's display to try to work out why it's not printing. Usually, there will be some error status listed against the job in the print queue, perhaps 'Paper Jam', or 'Low Ink'. If it's obvious what the problem is, try to fix at the printer end, by clearing the jam or replacing the ink cartridge.

Action 6

If the paper feeds through, and the printing head moves backwards and forwards, but nothing is printed, try replacing the ink cartridge. The printer may not have noticed it's empty.

Action 7

If your printer appears to be OK in Device Manager, but you still can't print a test page, try deleting it and reinstalling it. Open the **Printers And Faxes** window. Find your printer, right-click its icon and select **Delete**. Select **Server Properties** from the **File** menu, click the **Drivers** tab, and select your printer. Click **Remove** and confirm your decision, forcing Windows to extract a clean driver file. Shut down your PC and turn off the printer. Check cables, then turn the printer back on and wait until it indicates it's ready. Restart your PC. Microsoft Windows should locate and install the printer automatically. If not, check with the printer's manufacturer for updated installation or driver files. If there is an updated installation program, download it to your PC, click the **Start** menu, select **Run**, and navigate to the file to install it. If not, check the printer's documentation to see if there are special installation instructions and follow them. Otherwise, go to **Printers and Faxes** and click **Add Printer** (under **Printer Tasks** in the left pane – see Fig. 8). Follow the instructions to add the printer, allowing Microsoft Windows to detect the printer automatically. Provide either the updated driver files or the files you originally installed if Windows prompts for drivers. If you had a driver problem, your printer should now appear in Device Manager and be able to print a test page.

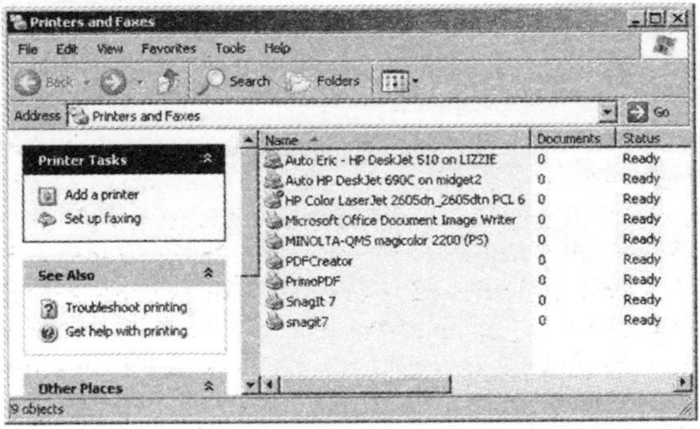

Fig. 8

If the test page prints but looks bad, you may have an ink or toner cartridge problem, or a paper problem. A bad test page is smudged, lined, patchy or has been ripped or folded by the printer mechanism. Using the right paper for your printer can improve printing quality as well as make paper pick-up and jam problems less likely. Sometimes different brands of paper can make a big difference, so it's worth trying. Paper should be clean, dry and unwrinkled, straight out of the packaging when you put it into your printer. Don't over-fill the blank paper hopper. If a paper change and a new ink or toner cartridge don't help, your printer is probably mechanically worn and needs replacement.

Action 8

If the ink and paper seem to be all right, you may be able to set the print quality in your application. Most applications allow you to adjust the printer properties. Usually there is a **Properties** button in a **Print Preview** or **Printer Settings** display (normally found in the **File** menu of the application) which will allow you to adjust the printer quality in a number of steps from Draft up to Best Photo (or similar names). If you can't find one, you can always go to **Start**-> **Control Panel**-> **Printers and Faxes**, right-click on your printer and select **Properties** (see Fig. 9). Click on **Display Properties** to show further details of the printer (see Fig. 10).

If you replace your printer with a new one, you should delete the old one from **Printers and Faxes**, as detailed above. Set your new printer to be the **Default Printer** on its **Properties** page.

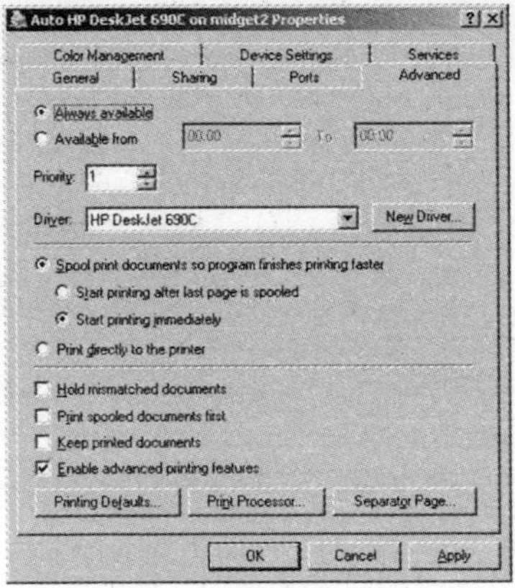
Auto HP DeskJet 690C on midget2 Properties
Color Management
Device Settings
Services
General
Sharing
Ports
Advanced
Always available
Available from
00:00
To
00:00
Priority: 1
Driver: HP DeskJet 690C
New Driver...
Spool print documents so program finishes printing faster
Start printing after last page is spooled
Start printing immediately
Print directly to the printer
Hold mismatched documents
Print spooled documents first
Keep printed documents
Enable advanced printing features
Printing Defaults...
Print Processor...
Separator Page...
OK
Cancel
Apply

Fig. 9

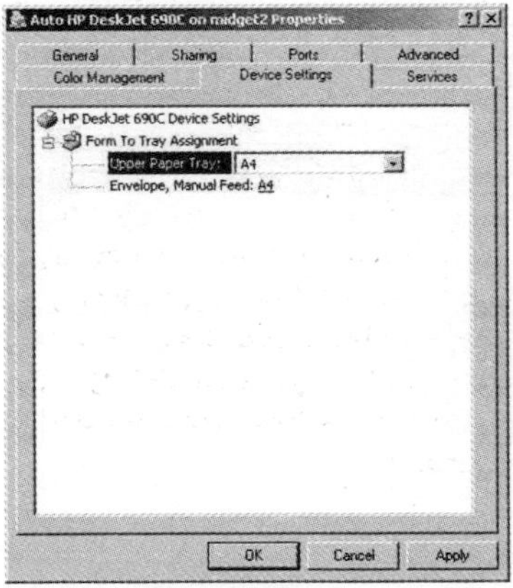
Auto HP DeskJet 690C on midget2 Properties
General
Sharing
Ports
Advanced
Color Management
Device Settings
Services
HP DeskJet 690C Device Settings
Form To Tray Assignment
Upper Paper Tray: A4
Envelope, Manual Feed: A4
OK
Cancel
Apply

Fig. 10

EXPERT TIP

If something major goes wrong inside the printer itself, you're probably best off disposing of the broken printer and buying a new one. Printers are very cheap these days, relatively speaking, and the cost of having an old one repaired can be almost as much as buying a new one, or even more.

Scanner

A scanner converts paper documents, paper photographs and sometimes slides, negatives and small three-dimensional objects into digital image form. Flatbed scanners have a horizontal glass plate on which you place the document to be scanned. Some scanners come with automatic document feeders, so you can load several pages into a document tray and have them scanned one after the other. Flatbed scanners, with fewer exposed moving parts, are usually more reliable. A document-feeding scanner often wears out in the same way as a printer.

Most scanners come with a CD of drivers, image-editing software and utilities to preview scans and set scan characteristics. If you haven't got the CD, look at the scanner for brand and model details, or find it in Device Manager under Imaging Devices, then find the manufacturer's website and download and install the programs you need for your model. It's a good idea to download the scanner's documentation and read it before you go any further.

EXPERT TIP

Although the scanner manufacturer will encourage you to install their own image-editing software and the like, make sure you really want and need it before installing anything. There's no point in installing their software if you're planning on using something different like Photoshop or GIMP.

Action 1

If your scanner doesn't appear in Device Manager, or won't scan, check for a shipping lock on the scanner. This is a mechanical lock designed to protect the delicate scanner mechanism during transit.

Action 2

If your scanner appears in Device Manager, go on to try to take a scan with the programs that came with it. If you have problems scanning, try installing the latest drivers from the manufacturer's website. If it still doesn't work, seek help on the Internet for your scanner model.

Action 3

If your scanner works, but the image quality it produces isn't as good as you'd like, first read the documentation to find out how to clean your scanner. If you have a document feeder, it may be becoming worn out.

Action 4

Check the scan settings in the supplied programs. You can usually adjust resolution, colour and brightness to improve the quality of scans. If the document you're scanning is printed on both sides, you may be experiencing bleed-through from the other side of the document. Once again, adjusting scan settings may help, or you can try putting a blank sheet behind the document you're scanning to help prevent bleed-through.

Multi-function device

If you're stuck for space around your PC, you may want to consider a multi-function device or MFD. This is essentially a printer and a scanner in one box. It can provide printing, scanning, copying and even fax services. Once you've got it running, you have the simplicity of using just one machine instead of three or four. The trade-off may be that if your MFD stops working, you lose all those functions at once.

Unfortunately, MFDs aren't as well supported by Microsoft Windows as printers are, so you may have to read manufacturers' instructions in detail and carefully follow them to install the necessary drivers correctly. Often, problems can be helped by obtaining the latest drivers from the manufacturer.

Action 1

If you've followed the instructions to the letter, but your MFD still doesn't show up in Device Manager, try another USB port. Some MFDs refuse to work with earlier generation USB ports. If you're thinking about buying an MFD, check your PC has appropriate USB ports for the model of MFD you're considering.

Action 2

If your MFD is supposed to provide fax services, you may need to plug it into a telephone line. Alternatively, it may be able to use a modem attached to your PC, in which case the modem will need to be compatible, correctly set up and plugged into a telephone line.

Action 3

As the MFD is a combined scanner and printer, you can experience a combination of the problems experienced by scanners and printers. Poor image quality is addressed in the same ways: cleaning, using the right paper and selecting quality settings in software.

Section 3: Cameras

Digital camera

Digital cameras are inexpensive and make taking photographs easy. Getting the photos onto your PC can be a challenge.

Some cameras are simplicity itself: just plug the supplied cable into a USB port on your PC, and the other end into the camera. Immediately, the camera appears as a mass storage device in Microsoft Windows with a drive letter and an icon of its own in My Computer, and you can copy the image files onto your hard drive for viewing and printing. Others may be more difficult.

If you have a camera without a suitable USB cable, try computer or camera shops. Take your camera to check you're getting the right cable.

The usual USB caveats apply: plug straight into your PC, avoiding external hubs, and try a different port if the first one doesn't work.

Action 1

Some cameras need to be set to a special mode before you can attach then to your PC. Some need to be turned on, and some need to be turned off. Read the instructions carefully to see whether this is the case.

Action 2

If you find your images are corrupted when they arrive on your PC, try changing your camera's batteries before you start transferring images.

Action 3

If your camera's batteries won't last long enough for you to transfer your images to your PC, consider buying a USB memory card reader. Your digital camera stores images on a flash memory card, which you can remove from the camera and plug into the memory card reader. Read your camera's instructions to find out how to remove the memory card. Since the memory card reader is powered by your PC's USB cable, you don't need to worry about the drain on your camera's batteries.

EXPERT TIP

When buying a new computer or multi-function device like a printer-scanner, you may find that it has a memory card reader built in. There are many different formats for memory cards, so if you get a built-in reader make sure it accepts the format your camera uses.

Action 4

Cameras may require drivers to be installed. Check with the manufacturer's documentation. If you have more than one camera, you can find that their drivers interfere with each other. You may see one camera never appearing at all, or success may depend on the order you attach the cameras. A reboot may let you use the cameras in series. In this situation, a memory card reader can be a good choice, since you won't need to install the cameras' drivers to access your images.

If you have a memory card reader, you can use it to format new memory cards for your camera. Check your camera's instructions to see which file system format to use. Cameras almost always require the FAT12 or FAT16 formats. We think it's always best to format your memory card in your camera, because it's guaranteed to use the right format. If your camera displays a message suggesting it doesn't recognise the memory card, follow the camera's instructions to format the card, as it may be in the wrong format. If that doesn't work, you probably have an incompatible or damaged memory card.

Webcam

Webcams are small digital cameras attached to your PC, almost always by USB. They're useful if you use instant messaging applications like Windows Messenger or Skype and you want your correspondents to be able to see you. Webcams come with various capabilities. Simple ones are fixed-focus cameras, whereas complicated ones can have software-controlled focus, pan, tilt and zoom. They can also be set up to take pictures driven by a timer, so you get a picture once a minute, say. If you have a website, you can upload the pictures to it so other people can share the view of the wildlife in your back garden, or whatever else of interest your webcam can see, in near-real time. For home security use, it's best to research specialised hardware with its own networking built in.

Recent webcams are usually plug and play. Just plugging one in is often enough to get your instant messenger application to ask you whether you want to use it. Older designs may require you to install drivers from a CD. If you need drivers, take care to follow the instructions supplied with the device, or search the manufacturer's website for details.

Action 1

Like other USB devices, if you experience problems eliminate any external USB hub, and try different USB ports on your PC. Simple webcams consume little power, so they're often good candidates to go on a USB hub, if you have one.

You can test your webcam by configuring your messaging application to use the device, or by using software that came with the webcam.

If you have a CD that goes with your webcam it will often have extra software to drive the camera in different ways that you might find useful.

Action 2

If your webcam stops working, and can no longer be found in Device Manager, the odds are it's a cable problem. If the cable looks good, try the webcam on another machine to see whether it works there.

Action 3

If the webcam appears in Device Manager but doesn't work in your application, you probably need to examine the application's settings and preferences to re-choose the device.

Section 4:
Modems and routers
(the Internet doesn't work)

When the Internet doesn't work for hardware reasons, you should first know how the Internet is supposed to be delivered to your PC. Usually, the Internet comes on cables, even if your PC is wireless. Deciding whether your cables are all plugged in the right places can be a challenge. There's also the possibility that one of the numberless series of cables outside your house between you and almost every other computer in the world is experiencing a problem.

Whatever system delivers your Internet access, you probably have a box called a modem or a router plugged into your provider's cable or phone socket. When you're looking at your modem and router cables, examine the plugs carefully for damage and discard the cable if there's any visible sign. Sometimes they don't survive being trodden on.

When debugging your Internet access, don't jump to the conclusion you have a hardware problem and start feverishly replugging cables. Communication services, even 'always on' services, are always unavailable for part of the time. If the lights are glowing on your modems and routers, first suspect the service is broken.

EXPERT TIP

A modem is a device that can actually communicate down a phone line or cable, while a router provides other facilities like wireless networking. If you have cable access, you may well have it plugged into the modem and then a router plugged into the modem to provide you with your local network.

Action 1

If your Internet service comes with your telephone line, check to see whether you have a dialling tone. If your router has an internal Web interface, you may be able to display the status of your line. Infrequent service disconnections for periods of up to an hour seem normal, but if disconnections become frequent you should contact your service provider to try to seek a resolution.

EXPERT TIP

Your broadband or cable supplier probably has telephone numbers you can ring to find out if there are problems on their end of the network. Make sure you write these down, as if there is a problem with the network in general, you won't be able to visit their website to find out.

Action 2

If you're disconnected for longer than an hour, you might like to ring your service provider to see whether they know what's going on. Parts of any large-scale cabled network are constantly being disrupted by mechanical diggers installing new cable, let alone all the other people let loose with mechanical diggers. Help desks are not always well informed about the low-level details of the networks for which they're responsible.

STUCK IN THE SLOW LANE

Waiting an hour to see if it's really broken or just a minor glitch may seem slow, but we say do everything to do with networking devices slowly. When you reset one end of an Internet service link, it's best to give the other end plenty of time to work out you've gone away, reset itself, and get ready to talk again when you turn the power on again at your end.

Your connection to the Internet probably arrives at your house on your telephone line. In some areas, you may have a cable provider who will supply television, telephone, Internet connectivity or all three services through a cable in your street. There's an outside chance your mobile phone provider has sold you a modem that connects through the mobile network.

You can use your telephone line to access the Internet in one of two ways. The older way is to use an analogue or 'dial-up' modem. This device makes a call on your telephone line, so you can't use the line for voice calls at the same time. The analogue modem dials a number, and another modem answers at the other end, if you got the number right. The two modems communicate by converting digital data into sound you can hear and sending it up and down the line. This severely limits the speed of communication.

In the last ten years, ADSL services have become widespread and affordable. The ADSL modem works by sending digital data up and down your telephone line at an inaudibly high frequency to special equipment in your local exchange. The speed of communication is much higher, you can use the line for voice calls at the same time, and the connection is always on – unlike an analogue modem where there's a boring delay while the call is connected and the two analogue modems get set up to talk to each other. A cable service is more or less the same as ADSL, but on different wiring. High-speed services like ADSL and cable offer higher or lower speeds, depending on exactly which technology your local provider offers.

EXPERT TIP

New ADSL2+ and LLU technologies are now appearing. These offer download speeds of up to three times that of normal ADSL and cable suppliers. If speed is important to you, it may be worthwhile checking to see if there is a supplier in your area, but as it requires physical changes to the BT exchange, it may well not be available in your area for a while.

Analogue modem

Your laptop or Desktop PC might have an analogue modem built in, an 'internal modem'. Take a look in Device Manager. If there's a modem that's got a yellow question mark next to it, you'll need to install a driver for it, probably from the PC manufacturer's CD or website. Check that the single cable between the modem/telephone socket on your laptop or Desktop PC is connected to a telephone socket with a dialling tone on it. Listen first with a normal telephone to verify the dialling tone. If things go badly later on, especially messages like 'no dial tone', try another cable and ideally another telephone socket before you give up. Modem cables are known to come in different types, so research to match up the cable you need with the modem you've got can pay dividends.

USB analogue modems are cheap and readily available. There will be two cables to check, one between the modem and a USB port on your PC, and one between the USB modem and the telephone socket on the wall. If you have problems connecting, check Device Manager and the modem cable, as described above for an internal modem.

RETRO TECH

While analogue modems sound like they're pretty much a thing of the past, we think they still have their place. Many analogue modem services still exist to permit access in areas where ADSL and cable haven't yet penetrated, to allow people on the move to connect to the Internet (ADSL and cable are tied to a specific phone line), and to provide a backup service for ADSL and cable. Your ADSL or cable provider may provide a dial-up service for you to use, or a

---

little research will turn up services you pay for by dialling a phone number at a local rate, often misleadingly called 'free'. They're certainly quite cheap, and unlike cable and ADSL, there's very little administration and service connection to go through to get the service set up. The best approach is to find out what services are available to you and follow their configuration instructions. If you're waiting for your ADSL or cable service to be delivered, trying your service provider's backup service is a good use of your time. When your 'always on' service is off for a while, at least you might be able to get your email. Don't expect YouTube to look good on an analogue modem, and the Web may seem very slow.

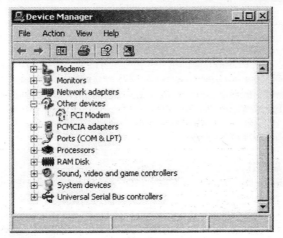

Fig. 11

Cable router/modem

This will be installed by your cable service company and will almost certainly have an Ethernet socket on it. If your PC really doesn't have an Ethernet socket, you might be able to beg a USB cable modem out of your service provider, but they'd much rather you used an Ethernet card, because it's much more reliable, cutting down on their support calls. High-speed USB drivers can suffer from stability and performance problems.

Choose an Ethernet cable if you can. You may get a wireless connection option.

Your service provider should have given you documentation about what the lights on your ADSL router/modem mean, but there should be a light on. If not, check its power cable and supply.

You should test with one Ethernet cable between your PC and the cable router/modem. If your router/modem has wireless connection, we recommend you test your Internet connection with an Ethernet cable if you can, to distinguish Internet service problems from wireless connection problems.

ADSL router/modem

Like cable Internet service, you're much better off with an Ethernet router/modem than a USB modem for ADSL.

ADSL has a further twist; it requires microfilters on your phone socket. Microfilters separate the normal phone signal from the ADSL signal coming down your phone line. Some wall sockets for phones will have integrated microfilters, in which case there will be two sockets in the box in the wall, one marked 'Phone' and the other 'ADSL'.

If you don't have integrated microfilters, then you should have a short cable with a normal phone plug on one end which plugs into the phone socket, and two sockets on the other end for your phone and your ADSL to plug into.

Action 1
If your ADSL connection isn't working, or keeps dropping out, you should check that there are correctly installed microfilters on everything attached to your telephone circuit. Handsets, faxes, analogue modems and satellite TV boxes all need to be plugged into the 'Phone' socket of the microfilter; your ADSL router modem should be the only thing plugged into a 'Modem' or 'ADSL' socket.

Action 2
If the telephone wiring on your side of the master socket looks at all ramshackle or excessively old, you might need to get a telephone engineer to look at it.

Action 3
If your router/modem has wireless connection, test your Internet connection with an Ethernet cable if you can to distinguish Internet service problems from wireless connection problems. You should test with one Ethernet cable between your PC and the cable router/modem.

Action 4
Your service provider should have given you any available documentation about what the lights on your ADSL router/modem mean, but there should be a light on. If not, check its power cable and supply.

For an ADSL connection there will be two or three cables: one Ethernet cable between your PC and the modem/router, a cable between the modem/router and either a dedicated ADSL socket on a wall plate or the modem side of a microfilter, and a short third cable connecting the microfilter to a telephone socket.

Action 5

If you're still having problems, try replacing the microfilters. You can buy a new one quite cheaply, and even if it doesn't solve the problem, it's always good to have a spare.

Mobile network

Your mobile network service provider will supply you with a modem, which will be a USB device, or a PC Card on a laptop. Any necessary drivers will come on a CD with instructions. As with all USB devices, if you get no response, check Device Manager, try another port and eliminate external hubs.

For the mobile connection there will be one USB cable or no cables at all. It's currently the most wireless you can get, though you can end up paying a lot of money for that freedom.

Network interface cards

Almost all modern PCs and laptops will have an Ethernet network interface card (NIC) built in. We love wired NICs. They do just one thing – ship network data around – and they usually do it very well. Lights flash to tell you whether the NIC is working. Wired NICs are outstandingly reliable, and their cables are cheap and easy to swap. Ethernet will run over a variety of cables, but the only one you're likely to see has plugs like larger telephone plugs at each end. These are called 'RJ-45's.

Wireless NICs can be more of a problem. You don't often see a maximum length Ethernet cable, at 1,500 feet, but it's quite easy to get out of range of your wireless router, or encounter long bursts of interference.

As usual, Device Manager will tell you whether your NIC is recognised and error free (see Fig. 12). If the lights flash on your wired NIC, it's almost certainly working. Any problems you have will be in software.

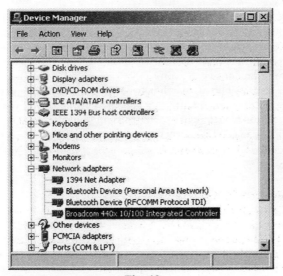

Fig. 12

Wireless NICs can be reliable when they're operated close to their base station. Persistent problems can be very difficult to diagnose for sure without an expensive survey. The easiest thing to change is the location of the router relative to the wireless PC (move it closer), but the outcome is often uncertain. If you can change the radio channel in use on the wireless router, this can also help. The documentation for the wireless router should tell you how to do this.

If you have more than one PC you might be using an Ethernet hub or switch. If you have an ADSL or cable modem/router it probably has a hub or switch built in – two or four RJ-45 sockets on the modem/router box. Hubs and switches let PCs talk to each other over Ethernet cables. Like NICs, they're usually very reliable, so if the power light is on, and the LEDs near the sockets flicker, your hub or switch is probably working. Still, if you have a separate hub or switch between you and your Internet access router/modem, it's a good idea to bypass it if you can, and plug straight in to the modem/router while you're trying to get the Internet working.

Chapter Four:
Software Problems

Software is complicated. No, *really* complicated. More complicated than pretty much anything else made by humankind. While this sounds like special pleading from disorganised software developers, it really is true. We're constantly amazed things work so well in software, not that they fail to work so often.

One of the reasons software is complicated is that all grown-up programs have some settings so the PC user can tailor the software to their taste. When things aren't working, it's very easy to lose track of what you've changed as you blunder around in a maze of dialog boxes. Remember to follow our advice from Chapter Two: be methodical, and keep track of what you've changed.

Section 1:
Operating system

The operating system is the layer of software that coordinates sharing the resources of your PC, like the screen, keyboard, mouse and disk, between the various application programs you run. Because it 'owns' the screen, keyboard and mouse, how it's set up can affect the usability of your PC a lot.

Most really serious problems with the Microsoft Windows operating system result in you being unable to use some, most or all of your PC. These can be complex to diagnose and recover from and we have addressed these areas in the first two chapters. In this section we cover some of the common *how to...* issues for Microsoft Windows. Microsoft provides extensive help, both on your PC and online, and it can all be accessed by clicking the **Start** button and then selecting **Help and Support**.

How do I change my Desktop settings?

Almost everything to do with your Desktop can be configured by right-clicking anywhere on the Desktop and selecting **Properties** (in Vista, **Personalize**). For all the Desktop settings, you can change them and click the **Apply** button in the Properties dialog box to see what the changes look like. If you don't like the changes, just set them back again.

● **The Themes** tab (see Fig. 1) allows you to select and save different combinations of window appearance, screen saver, background and so on. When you've got a combination of screen saver, background and window appearance you like you can save this by clicking the **Save As** button and giving the theme a name so you can easily restore your combination in the future.

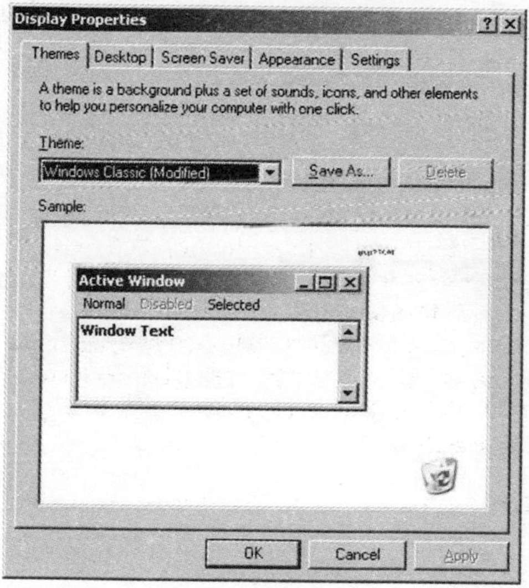

Fig. 1

- **The Desktop** tab (see Fig. 2 or Fig. 3 for Vista) allows you to change the picture displayed as the background on your Desktop. You can choose from a set of provided pictures, or choose any picture saved on your disk drive. If you see a picture while browsing the web that you think you'd like, just right-click on it and select **Set As Desktop Background**. If the picture isn't the same size as your display resolution, you can set its position to **Center** (doesn't change the size, just puts the middle of the picture in the middle of the screen), **Tile** (puts the top left of the picture in the top left of the screen and repeats down and across the screen to fill it), or **Stretch** or **Fit to Screen** (squishes and/or stretches the picture so it fits exactly – unless your picture has the same height:width ratio as your screen this can be less than pretty).

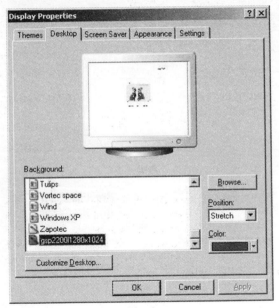

Fig. 2

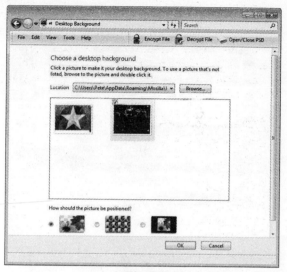

Fig. 3

- **The Appearance** tab (see Fig. 4) allows you to set
  the general appearance of the windows: the colour of
  the title bar, appearance of buttons, size of fonts and
  the like. Be warned when setting size of fonts – not all
  applications respect this setting, and may only show a
  larger font in the title bar.

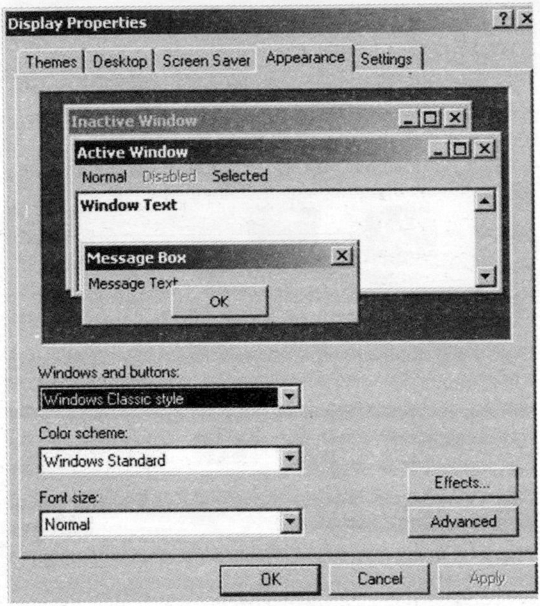

Fig. 4

- **The Settings** tab allows you to change the screen resolution and colour palette. This is a bit more technical than the other options (see Screen, Section 1 of Chapter Three).

My icons and applications are the wrong size

The first thing to check for size problems is your screen resolution (see Screen, Chapter Three). If you're using an inappropriate screen size (like 800x600 pixels on a 1,920x1,200 pixel screen or vice versa) everything on the screen can appear large and blocky or very small.

If the resolution is OK, you've probably accidentally activated the Microsoft Ease of Use settings. These settings allow for display of very large fonts and icons for the partially sighted or even a narrator for the blind. They also include things like using your computer without a keyboard, mouse or screen. If you have a disability which makes a normal computer hard to use, then these settings are something you want to turn on, but generally you will want them all turned off. To change or check these settings, select **Start->Control Panel->Accessibility Options** (or for Vista, **Ease of Use**).

PEBCAK

When technical support engineers chat, you'll sometimes hear PEBCAK problems mentioned. This is an acronym for Problem Exists Between Chair And Keyboard, which is to say the PC user themselves took some action, maybe changing some settings, to create the problem. Often it'll be the technical support engineer describing their own activities. We all experience PEBCAK moments.

The time is always wrong on my computer

Assuming you (or an annoying person) haven't set the time wrong on purpose, and assuming whatever clock you're checking the time against is actually right itself, then this is probably down to the fact that PCs, like watches, don't keep perfect time. In fact, there are only a few clocks in the world that keep perfect time, and they only do it because 'perfect time' is defined as the time those clocks keep.

However, you can fix all these problems and have your computer keep time as if it had an atomic clock installed. Right-click on the clock at the bottom right of the Taskbar and select **Adjust Date/Time**. The displays are different between XP and Vista, but the options are all there. Just click around until you find the one you want – the worst you can do is set your time wrong, and we've already established it's not right. The options you can set are:

● **Date and Time**

● **Time Zone** – if your time is an exact number of hours off, you're probably set to the wrong time zone already.

● **Internet Time** – if you constantly reset your clock and find it's wrong a week or two later, it's probably because you haven't ticked the box that tells your computer to use Internet time. Checking this box (see Fig. 5) means your computer will periodically check with an online server that provides the correct time, which it gets from an atomic clock. If this is checked on your PC, we recommend you take your watch in to the jeweller and get it cleaned.

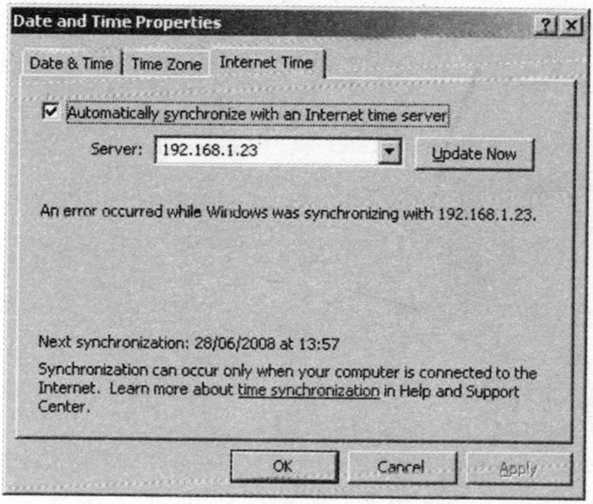

Fig. 5

- (Vista Only) **Additional Clocks** – a very useful option in this day and age of Auntie Vera living in Australia, which allows you to set up a couple of additional clocks for different time zones. If you set these, then when you hover your mouse over the clock on the Taskbar you can see the time in several different places at once, and time your phone calls to ensure you don't get Vera out of bed in the middle of the night.

My Desktop icons are broken

Sometimes you may find the icons on your Desktop lose their pretty picture or won't run the application they're meant to. The usual cause for this is that the icon has been deleted or the program has been moved.

Action 1

If the icon has lost its picture but still starts the application, right-click on the icon and select **Properties**. Click on the **Change Icon** button. This should show the current icon and may allow you to choose from several options. You can use the **Browse** button to search your disk for another icon (.ico file) – good places to look are the Applications folders, and selecting the application program file itself (.exe) may offer you a bunch of choices.

Action 2

If the application won't start when you double-click on its Desktop icon, make sure it's still installed. The **Properties** window for the icon will show the name of the application file, and if you click **Open File Location** you should open a Windows Explorer window showing the applications directory. Make sure the file is still there. If it is, then you may have a problem with the application itself. If it's not there, did you un-install it or upgrade to a new version which sits in a different folder?

Action 3

If you can't get the icon to work at all, try clicking **Start->All Programs** and finding the **Applications** folder. If you right-click on the application there and select **Send To Desktop** you can create a new icon and then just delete the broken one.

How do I set my PC up for power saving?

Power-saving options allow the PC to send various devices to sleep for a while when they're not being used. This is good for saving power, and thus good for both the environment and your wallet. If you want to set these up, many newer PCs have special applications for doing this (check the documentation that came with your PC), but you can always find them by clicking **Start->Control Panel -> Power Options** (see Fig. 6 or Fig. 7 for Vista).

Many of the options will vary from PC to PC and operating system to operating system. Usually you will have a selection of schemes called names like 'Power Saver' (for the eco-aware among you) and High Performance (the dilithium crystals won't take it, Cap'n). You can create your own schemes as well, deciding for yourself when you want the computer to turn off the screen or disk drives, or hibernate completely.

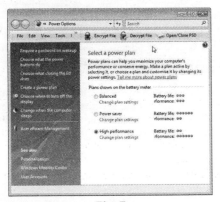

Fig. 6

Fig. 7

If you reduce your power consumption a lot there are obvious benefits, but if you do it too soon or too much you may find yourself waiting a lot when you come back to your PC while it grinds back into action. These things are all really a matter of taste, so experiment and find something that fits the way you work.

I think my registry is broken

Your PC is acting 'completely crazy'. Is the registry broken?

All we can say is, 'If it is, you're in a lot of trouble'. The registry is a file that Windows uses to hold its really important information about your PC, Microsoft Windows itself and applications you run. If it is broken or corrupt, or has been sabotaged by some piece of malware, it can have very serious repercussions throughout your system. In some cases parts or all of your PC may be unusable.

There is a program you can run to edit registry entries by hand and there are programs you can use to fix the registry when it's broken. However, we're not going to tell you about them because this procedure should only be performed by someone who knows exactly what they're doing, as any mistake could make matters much, much worse. If you really do want to try doing this on your own, make sure you back up everything first and then use Google to find out more about the process. But we don't recommend tinkering with the registry unless you're an expert.

If you do suspect a broken registry, then our recommended approach is:

Action 1

Immediately back up your system and set up a new System Restore Point (see Section 1 of Chapter One) before anything gets any worse.

Action 2

If feasible, try restoring from a previous System Restore Point and see if that fixes the problem.

Action 3

If it's still broken, or if you didn't want to do a System Restore because you haven't been taking backups regularly and you'd just lose too much data, then either try re-installing Windows, or contact an expert.

Photos look good on the screen, but bad when I print

This is a fairly common problem. The picture looks fine on the screen, but when you print you get horizontal lines across it, or it's blurry and blotchy, or the colours are all wrong. The first thing to check is that you're using a suitable type of paper. You won't get photo quality printing if you're using recycled paper.

Action 1

If the picture prints, but is blurry and blotchy, chances are it's been blown up to too large a size. Some applications default to printing a picture the same size as the paper. If it's smaller than the piece of paper to begin with, then the software guesses what colour the extra pixels should be, and it's not very good at that. Unless you have very sophisticated image processing software, life is not like *CSI*: when you blow up the small indecipherable face on the security camera picture, what you actually get is a bigger, more indecipherable face. Try printing the picture from the application by choosing **File->Print** (so it doesn't just print straight away and gives you an option window instead) and look to see if there's a **Fit to page** check box or an **Image Size** option that's set to 300 per cent. Try unchecking the box or select 100 per cent instead.

Action 2

If the picture has horizontal lines or banding, you're probably printing in what's called draft quality. Draft quality is good for checking prints are correct because they don't use much ink, but for good pictures you need something better. Again, click **File->Print** in the application and see if there's a quality setting. For pictures, you want **Photo Quality** (or **Best Photo Quality**). If you don't see a quality option, try clicking **Properties** next to the box where you select the printer. You may also have a control on your printer itself that allows you to set the print quality.

Action 3

If you still have problems, try printing a test page on your printer (either from the printer's software options window, or using controls on the printer). If that looks bad, then check the ink levels and maybe try cleaning the printing heads (again, using the printer's software properties or controls on the printer itself).

Action 4

If the picture is printed in the wrong colours, you could be running low on ink, or the colour palette your printer and application are using are wildly different. It's beyond the scope of this book to try and deal with printing colour palettes, so check your application, screen and printer documentation.

If none of these work, you may have a printer problem (see Printer, Section 2 of Chapter Three).

My CDs won't/always run automatically

CD and DVD drives can be set to run a program automatically when the disk is inserted in the drive. Some people think this is a good thing. Others, who prefer more control, don't like it. You can't control what program is run (that's defined by options on the CD itself), but you can decide what happens when you insert the disk.

To set these options on (or off), you need to find them first. In Windows XP, open **Windows Explorer** (see File System in Section 2 of this chapter if you're not familiar with Windows Explorer) and then right-click on the drive in the list of disk drives and choose **Properties**. Then select the **Auto Play** tab. In Vista, you need to click **Start->Control Panel ->AutoPlay**.

Once you've found the options, you can select what you want to happen when you insert a CD. This can be anything from nothing to auto-running the CD or opening specific applications depending on the type of CD. Choose your poison as you prefer.

Multimedia or QuickLaunch keys don't work

Keyboards at the higher end of the market (and many newer laptops) often come with special keys that control your media player, open email applications or web browsers and start instant messaging applications. As time goes on, more are being added to this list. However, often you may find that pressing these fantastically useful keys does nothing.

Action 1

Most keyboards like this come with special applications software to set up and control these keys. If you didn't install the software when you plugged in your keyboard (and it's entirely likely you didn't, as Windows will automatically recognise and use the rest of the keyboard), then do so. It should be on the start-up disk that came with the keyboard. Open the application and check that the keys are all turned on and configured correctly.

Action 2

If the keys seem to be configured correctly and still don't work, the software that came with your keyboard may well be out of date. Try downloading the latest version of the keyboard application software and keyboard drivers from the manufacturer's website.

Action 3

If you're using a non-Windows media player such as Winamp, you may find that by default the keyboard is not supported. But if you check the media player's website and search on Google, you may find a plug-in bit of software or a widget you can install which will make them work properly.

Action 4

If you still have problems, you may never get them to work. The same applies if you're using a KVM switch (a device which allows you to use one keyboard, mouse and screen shared between multiple computers), and sometimes when using wireless keyboards. Check the packaging and documentation that came with the hardware to make sure the version of the operating system you're using is supported. If it claims to be, try asking at the shop you bought it from, or sending an email to the manufacturer's support department. Remember to make notes on exactly what model of keyboard you're using, what version of the operating system you have, and the version of the keyboard application software you're running.

Characters repeat when I type

Keyboards are designed to repeat a key a number of times when you hold it down. If this is happening when you just touch the key lightly, you need to check your keyboard configuration.

Action 1

Click **Start->Control Panel->Keyboard**. Find the option that deals with **Repeat Delay** (see Fig. 8). This controls how long it waits after you press the key before it starts repeating it. Adjust until you get a setting you like.

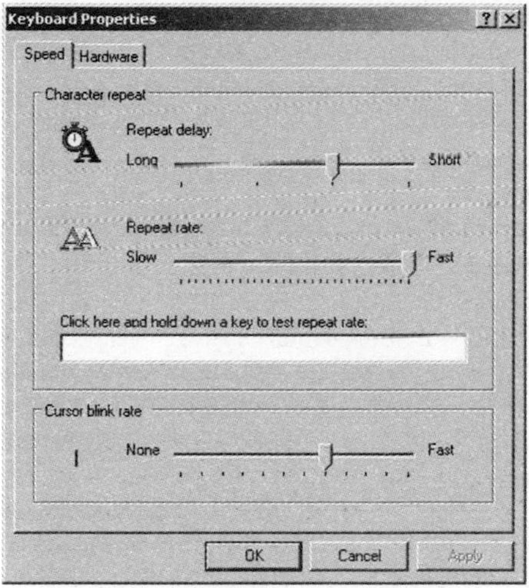

Fig. 8

Action 2

If changing the settings makes no difference, then you may have a dirty or broken keyboard.

My keyboard doesn't type the right characters

The first possibility is that some bright spark has swapped the keys on your keyboard as a practical joke, but the more likely possibility is that your keyboard is set to some funny configuration. Different countries have different keyboard layouts and Windows can be set for any of them.

A common problem is that your computer was set up for a US keyboard when it was delivered. If you get a $ sign instead of a £ when you type, and your " and @ keys are swapped, then you're using a US keyboard with a UK keyboard layout.

Action 1

Click **Start->Control Panel->Regional and Language Options**. Select the **Keyboard** tab, and check that the setting matches your actual keyboard. You can also access this menu via a small button labelled EN which may be displayed on your Taskbar, and is also shown on the log on screen when you start up Windows (useful for when you want to change your keyboard set up before you sign on).

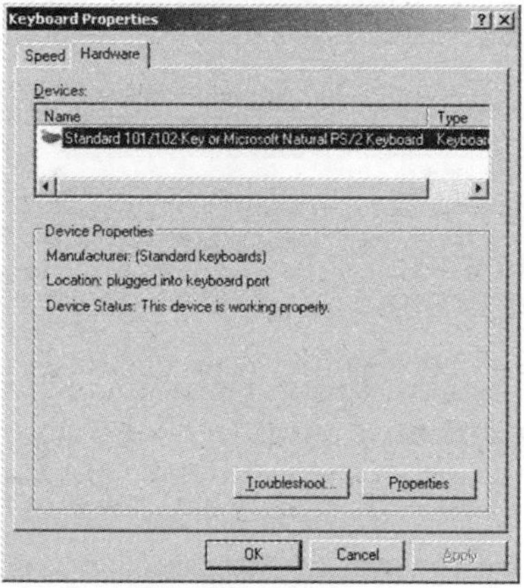

Fig. 9

Action 2

If you travel internationally a lot and like to use a bigger local keyboard instead of the keyboard on your laptop, you get the EN menu to appear on your Taskbar all the time by making sure the **Hide the Language Bar** option is not checked in the **Regional and Language Options**. This allows you to change keyboard layouts with only two clicks.

StickyKeys is turned on/off

StickyKeys is an ease-of-use option you can set up to make it easier to hold down combinations of keys (like Ctrl+Alt+Del – no, don't try that now). Sometimes when pressing keys together Windows will ask you if you want to turn StickyKeys on. If you want to turn them on or off, or adjust their settings, these options can be found by clicking **Start->Control Panel->Accessibility Options** (or for Vista, **Ease of Use**).

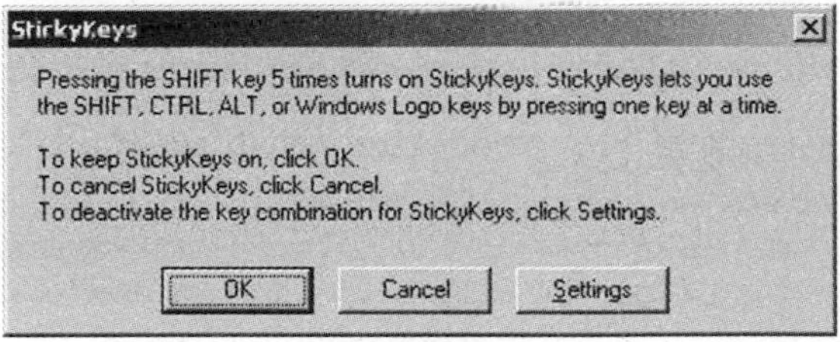

StickyKeys	☒
Pressing the SHIFT key 5 times turns on StickyKeys. StickyKeys lets you use the SHIFT, CTRL, ALT, or Windows Logo keys by pressing one key at a time.	
To keep StickyKeys on, click OK.	
To cancel StickyKeys, click Cancel.	
To deactivate the key combination for StickyKeys, click Settings.	
OK Cancel Settings	

Fig. 10

How do I get rid of an application?

When you've downloaded an application to try it out and decided you don't want it after all, or an old application is no longer any use, you will probably want to delete it to free up space on your disk and get rid of unwanted entries in your Start menu. The first rule is DON'T just find the program on your hard drive and delete the folder. That often leaves a half-installed mess.

Action 1

Most applications provide a method of removing themselves. For normal applications, click on **Start->All Programs**, find the application folder entry and see if there's an uninstall program provided. This is the best and cleanest way of getting rid of a program, as the uninstall program will not only delete the application and its folders, it will also clean up registry entries and get rid of data it's left in various other folders scattered round your drive. You may be presented with options like repairing, removing or changing application features. Just select what it is you want to do and follow the on-screen instructions.

Action 2

If there is no uninstall program provided, click on **Control Panel->Add or Remove Programs** (Vista: **Programs and Features**). This will open a window with a list of all the applications installed on your machine. Select the undesired application and click **Remove** or **Uninstall** and follow the on-screen instructions.

EXPERT TIP

If you want to add or remove features from Windows itself,
look for **Add/Remove Windows Features/Components**
on the left-hand side of the **Add/Remove Programs**
window.

Action 3

If the application isn't in the Control Panel uninstall
list, then there are a couple of options. Some very small
applications don't actually go through the Windows
install process. When you download them they just have
instructions that say something like 'Create a directory,
unzip the file and click on the .exe file'. If you remember
this was the case then just track down the folder you installed
the program into using Windows Explorer and delete the
folder. However, if it did go through the normal install
process and doesn't appear to have any method of removing,
it's probably because the program is (or contains) some piece
of malware that is doing whatever it can to prevent itself
being uninstalled. In this case you revert to a Restore Point
prior to the software being installed.

Section 2:
File system

Your disk drive is one of the most important parts of your
computer. In the hardware chapter we discussed various
problems that may occur with the drive itself, but you
may also run across things that cause you problems even

though the disk is functioning perfectly. However, before we charge headlong into what goes wrong with the file system, it's important that you understand how your PC organises the files on your disk drive.

The tree of files

We're not going to delve into the mysteries of how files are actually stored on the disk. That's far too much information, and not really useful in day-to-day situations. What you do need to understand is the way the file system appears to you. Windows (and Linux) present the file organisation in what is called a 'tree view'.

A tree view looks nothing like a tree, but it's actually not a hard thing to visualise. Essentially, you start at ground level with what is known as a 'root' folder, called root because it's at the bottom of the tree. Into this folder, the PC puts other folders (think of these as branches) and files (leaves). And it gives each folder and file a name so they can be identified.

Now, into a branch folder it can put more folders (small branches) and files. This can go on forever – as long as there's a folder it can always contain more folders and files. The only limit is the physical amount of space on your disk.

Now, imagine turning this tree on its side so the root is on the left and the branches on the right. That's a tree view.

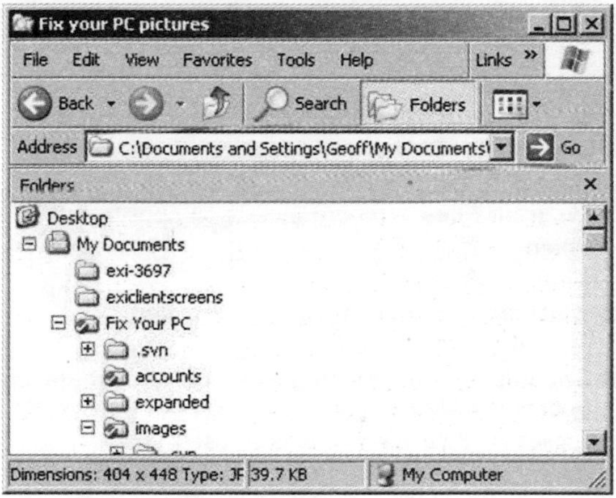

Fig. 11

As you can see in Fig. 11, on the left we have our root folder (C:), and it contains a whole bunch of other folders (like Program Files) and files. Because there can be a huge number of folders, it can be difficult to see them all at once, so Windows contracts the view so you only see those which are in the folder you're viewing. It indicates there are more folders contained in these folders by putting a + sign next to them. If you click on a + it expands that folder so you can see what's in it. Ad infinitum.

This logical view of files and folders on the disk is something you'll run across constantly on your PC, but you're usually seeing it from inside the Open File or Save File dialogs, where it's not always so obvious what's going on. Just remembering where you left things in a large tree of files can be a challenge.

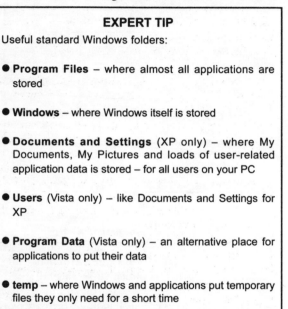

EXPERT TIP

Useful standard Windows folders:

- **Program Files** – where almost all applications are stored

- **Windows** – where Windows itself is stored

- **Documents and Settings** (XP only) – where My Documents, My Pictures and loads of user-related application data is stored – for all users on your PC

- **Users** (Vista only) – like Documents and Settings for XP

- **Program Data** (Vista only) – an alternative place for applications to put their data

- **temp** – where Windows and applications put temporary files they only need for a short time

Your friend the Explorer

Windows Explorer is an application which comes as an integral part of Windows and is among the most useful and least understood (by most people) pieces of software. When you open My Documents – that's really Windows Explorer.

So are the Control Panel, My Pictures, Network Places and many of the windows displayed by Browse buttons.

Unfortunately, Microsoft conceals much of the usefulness of Windows Explorer with pretty icons and fancy menu bars – partly to hide a very powerful tool from people who might easily break their PC by doing something dumb.

It's extremely worthwhile getting to know Windows Explorer. To open it, just click **Start->Programs->Accessories->Windows Explorer** (see Fig. 12). If you're using the default Windows set up, you'll see a panel with files and folders on the right and a panel on the left with a bunch of links. Although these links can be useful for the new user, we recommend changing the panel on the left to show you the tree view. On XP you can just click the **Folder** button near the top of the window. In Vista, click on the bar that says Folders with a little up arrow at the bottom of the links panel.

We strongly recommend you do not touch anything in the folders called Windows (where Windows is stored) or Program Files (where all applications should be stored) unless you really know what you're doing. But by all means have a poke around and see what's there. If you're familiar with the general structure of things on disk, it will make your life much easier when deciding what to back up, where to look for files and so on.

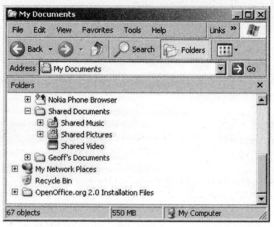

Fig. 12

I can't open a file

The most likely cause for this problem is that you're trying to access a file which belongs to someone else, either a shared file on the network or a file owned by another user on your PC. The owner of the file can restrict your access to their files on a number of different levels. You can ask them if they'll share it, but if they won't you have to respect their privacy.

If the problem file is one of yours, then the problem is almost certainly with the application. Check Applications in Section 5 of this chapter and Chapter Two.

I can't change a file

If you're trying to save a file and Windows won't let you, the file is probably opened in what is called Read Only mode. This means you can read it, but not change it. Some applications tell you when they open a file in Read Only mode, and some don't. There are a number of reasons why a file might be in Read Only mode.

Action 1

If the file is shared, someone else on the network has the file open as well. Most applications won't let two people write to the same file at the same time. Click on **Start**, then right-click on **My Computer** and select **Manage**. Select **System Tools->Shared Folders->Open Files** and see if the file is listed. If so, someone else is using it and you should check with them before trying to save your version.

Action 2

The file may be set to be always Read Only. This can be intentional, but can often happen when you've copied the file from a CD to your hard disk. To check, find the file in Windows Explorer, right-click on it and select **Properties**. If the **Read Only** box is checked (see Fig. 13), then you can set it to be writeable by unchecking the box. Be careful – make sure there isn't a good reason for it to be Read Only before you change it.

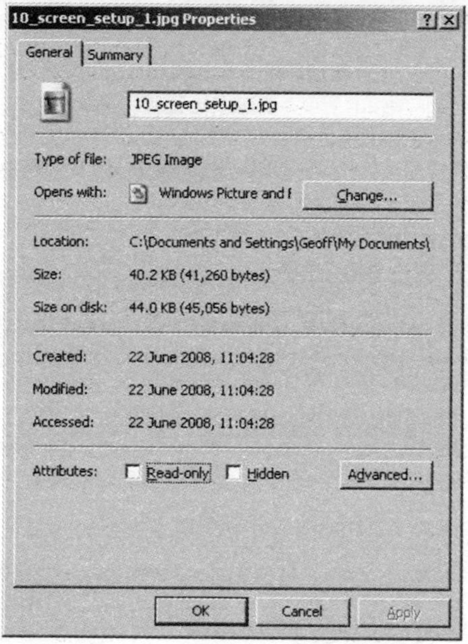

Fig. 13

Action 3

If the file is on someone else's computer in a network, you may not have permission to change the file. Check with the owner of the file if you'd like them to change things to allow you to write the file, but it's likely they may not want to do that.

Action 4

If the file is a Windows system file, Windows may not let you change it. This can be circumvented (in Vista) by running your application in Administrator mode (which you may not be allowed to do if it's not your PC). If this is the case, it's best not to touch the files unless you really know what you're doing.

I can't delete a file

Sometimes when you delete a file or folder, Windows tells you that it is in use and cannot be deleted. Generally speaking, if it's in use, then it's not a good idea to delete it.

Action 1

Check and see if the file is open in one of your applications. If so, then just close the application and try again.

Action 2

If you can't see the file open in any application, it may be opened by another user (if it's a shared file), or a system application or Windows itself. If the former, ask the other person to close their application, but if the latter it's almost always best to just leave the file where it is. Deleting files being used by the system can have serious repercussions.

Action 3

If the file is part of a software package you've just removed, you may need to reboot your PC before you're allowed to delete it.

Action 4

If you still can't get at the file, try starting in Safe Mode and trying from there.

Action 5

As a last resort, there are a number of software packages which will allow you to bypass the system security and delete the file regardless, such as MoveOnBoot (see Useful Resources). You should always use extreme caution when doing this as it may well cause other problems on your PC, but with some files installed by a virus there may be no other way.

I've deleted a file I want

One of the commonest problems is that you delete a file, the PC asks you if you're sure and you click yes without thinking. Oops. Or maybe you thought you wouldn't need it and find out later that you do.

Action 1

Windows actually just moves deleted files to a special folder called the Recycle Bin (see Fig. 14). Click on the **Recycle Bin** icon on your Desktop (or in Windows Explorer) and find the file you want. Right-click on it and select **Restore**. Hey presto! It's back where it was.

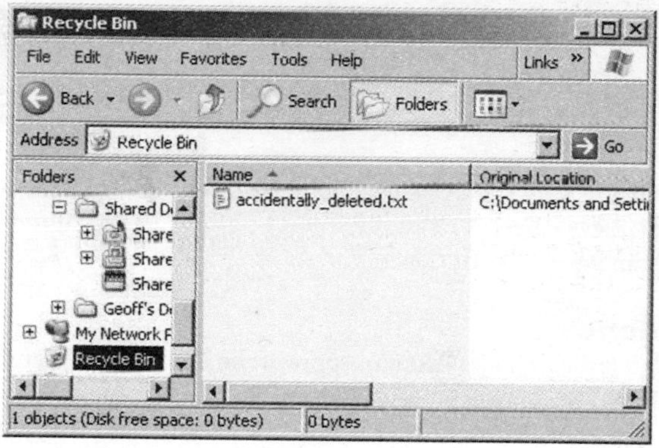

Fig. 14

Action 2

If you've emptied your Recycle Bin, or the deleted file was too large for Windows to put it there, then your best option is to go to a backup you made and restore the file from that.

Action 3

No backup? How embarrassing. Windows reuses disk space from deleted files, and the longer ago the file was deleted the less chance you have of the data still existing on your disk. However, you can install one of a large number of utility packages which will try and recover the data from your disk. Good luck – the process is far from guaranteed.

I've lost track of a file

If you can't find a file, it may have been deleted (see above). However, sometimes when you save a file the application saving it does so by default to some odd directory somewhere – it's easy not to notice where it is. Or possibly someone else using your PC just moved it. In these cases, Windows Explorer has a search facility to scan your disk for files.

Action 1

When searching, select an appropriate directory to search from by viewing it in Windows Explorer. If you have no idea where it might be, just select the root folder on your C drive, but if you can narrow it down, then you can save some time. Searching a large drive can take a long time.

Action 2

In XP, click **Start-> Search**, then select **All Files and Folders** from the links in the left-hand panel (see Fig. 15). Type the name of the file (or part of the name) into the file name box and click **Search**. If you don't find it you can always widen the search by looking for a smaller part of the name or changing it to a different directory. In Vista, there is a short cut for all this by typing the name of the file in the search box at the top of the window.

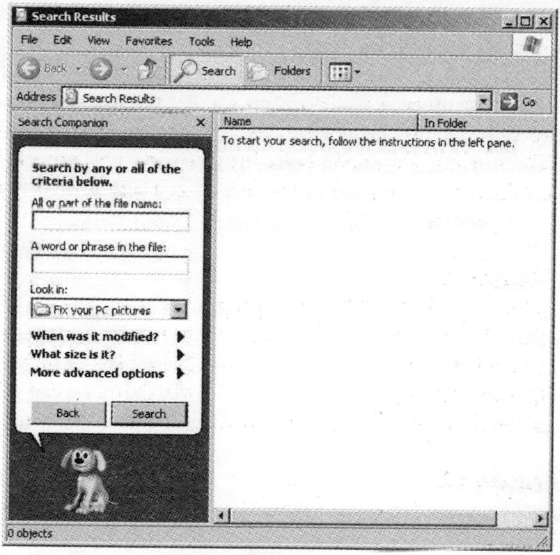

Fig. 15

EXPERT TIP

If you're sure you saved a file, but now you can't find it, open the application you used to make the file, and look in its Recent Files list. If that doesn't help, try saving an empty document – applications usually remember the last place they saved a file, and will open the Save dialog at that point. This time, note carefully where in the file tree the application's saving the file, then cancel the Save dialog.

The file is opening in the wrong application

Sometimes when you double-click on a file in Windows Explorer, a different application from the one you expected will open up. Windows associates file extensions (the .xxx at the end of the file name) with different applications: for example, .doc is usually associated with Word, but if you have Open Office it may be associated with Writer.

The associations usually change without your knowing it when you install a new application. If you install a new media player for Internet Explorer, it may automatically associate all media types with itself rather than your preferred media player. This can be enormously annoying and it's pretty naughty of the application to do it without asking you, but that's life.

Action 1

One way of resetting file associations is to go into your preferred application and look at its **Options** or **Preferences**. Most applications have some option to set them to open certain types of files.

Action 2

If that fails, open **Windows Explorer** and select **Tools-> Folder Options**, then select the **File Types** tab. Scroll down the list to select the three-letter extension of the file in question, click the **Change** button and choose the application you want as illustrated in Fig. 17. In Vista, right-click on the file and select **Open With-> Choose Default Program** to set the association. If you want to change the association for all files of the same type, click

the box at the bottom. Opening an unknown file brings
up this dialog.

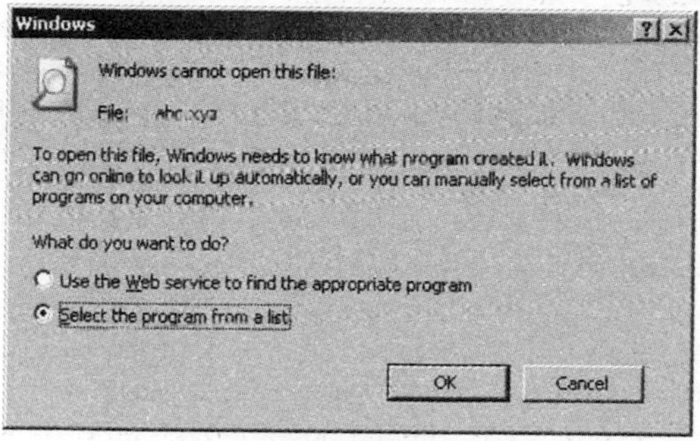

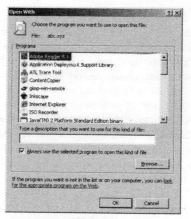

Fig. 16

Fig. 17

My disk is full

Even in these days of ever-expanding disks, you may still find a way to fill yours up ('Hey, have you seen my collection of every song ever recorded since the dawn of time?'). Aside from options like buying a new big drive to supplement or replace your old one, there are a few steps you can take to reduce the amount of junk (sorry, valuable data) you have on your disk.

Action 1

Empty the Recycle Bin. Just right-click on the **Recycle Bin** icon on your Desktop and select **Empty**. If there's the possibility you might want any of those deleted files you can always have a quick look through the bin first, but this action alone might save you a lot of space.

Action 2

Right-click on the drive in **Windows Explorer**, select **Properties** (see Fig. 18). This shows how much free space you have and how much you've used, and also has a **Disk Cleanup** button. There's a short delay while Windows looks for stuff it can delete (and Vista asks you whose files you want to delete as well), and then you get a window listing different types of files you might want to bin, and how much room they'll each save. Downloaded Programs, Temporary Internet, Recycle Bin, and Temporary Files are always good candidates. Tick the ones you want to ditch and click OK.

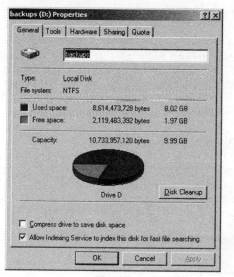

Fig. 18

Action 3

If you're still short of room, consider backing up seldom-used files to CD and deleting them off your hard drive, or deleting unused programs (see How do I get rid of a program? in Section 1 of this chapter).

I want to share some files

Do you? Fair enough, but be warned: sharing files or folders on your disk can be a security exposure. We advise you to read Shared files, Chapter One, Section 3 first. If you still want to share your files, then the best thing to do is copy files you want to share to your Shared Documents folder. For this go to **Start-> Windows Explorer-> Documents and Settings-> All Users-> Documents** (see Fig19). This folder is automatically set up by Windows for this very purpose.

If you find that you want to share a large amount of files (maybe you live in the vain hope that your kids might find your music collection interesting) you may be better off sharing the folder itself.

Fig. 19

Action 1

Right-click on the folder in **Windows Explorer** and select **Sharing and Security** (or just **Share** in Vista) (See Fig. 2). XP and Vista differ quite a lot in setting up sharing, but they have the same basic elements. Options include giving the shared folder a special name others will see on the network, setting whether users can change and add files in your shared folder, and whether you want to share the files with users on just your computer or the entire network.

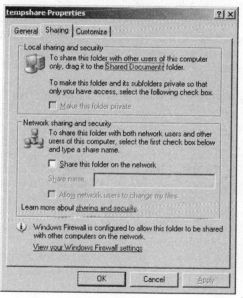

Fig. 20

We're not going to go through all the options, but we highly recommend you read the advice and instructions Microsoft gives. You can find informational and instructional links scattered across all the sharing windows.

EXPERT TIP

Never share a whole drive or root directory (unless the whole drive is dedicated to your music, for example), and certainly never share an entire drive or root directory allowing users to change it. Unless you really want someone to reformat the whole drive for you.

I've shared some files I don't want to

Well, we did warn you. Read 'I want to share some files' above and just uncheck and reset anything you set there.

My network drive isn't connecting

Network drives are shared folders or drives on your network which appear in Windows Explorer as drives attached to your own PC. This can be very useful if you access a shared drive frequently. You can set up a network drive by selecting **Tools->Map Network Drive** from the Explorer menu. Then you assign a drive letter (best to start with Z and work backwards) and click the Browse button to find the desired folder or drive on the network. If you click the **Reconnect at Login box**, the drive will now always appear as your Z (or whatever) drive in Windows Explorer. However, you may often see a small balloon saying some network drives were not reconnected when you log on to your computer.

Action 1

Check the computer the network drive is physically attached to is turned on and running. It probably isn't, in which case get it turned on, or just sigh and wait until someone else does.

Action 2

If the computer is on, check you're connected to the network. Can you Google? Can you see the computer in Network in Windows Explorer? Maybe the other computer is turned on, but it's network connection isn't working.

Action 3

If both computers are turned on and can see each other, try disconnecting the drive (right-click on it in Explorer and select **Disconnect**), and then re-map the drive.

Section 3:
Internet and networking

Access to the Internet is a prime reason for PC use. The necessary communication can be provided by telephone line, cable, public wireless LAN, mobile phone network, satellite or even stranger things like packet radio. For most of these services, there is a service provider who you need to reach a prior agreement with to supply the service.

Connecting

Whatever service provides your Internet connection, you may need a user ID and password, called your service credentials, to identify yourself to the service. If you're using a wireless network, there may be further credentials and settings, called your wireless credentials. The service credentials will be supplied by your service provider; the wireless credentials may need to be configured in your wireless router or access point, usually using a web-based control application in the router.

Going wireless

There are lots of ways to set up your wireless LAN and, unfortunately, the simplest isn't usually the best.

Your wireless router or access point will have a name, called an SSID, set for it. The simplest thing is to broadcast the name so everyone with a wireless NIC can see it. The best thing is not to do that, so your wireless network doesn't appear in the list of available networks.

Your wireless router or access point will have some level of encryption set (including no encryption). The simplest thing is to have no encryption, the best thing is to have the strongest encryption turned on. Often the complete encryption details are several words like 'WPA-PSK AES shared key: pennylane!beatles' which you need to note carefully, and make sure the settings in the router and your PC correspond.

Each wireless network card in a PC has a unique 'MAC address'. Your wireless router or access point will probably have a way of filtering by MAC address, so it'll only let certain MAC addresses use your network. The simplest thing is not to filter by MAC address. The best thing is to limit the PCs using your wireless network by MAC address.

If you're setting up from scratch, it's best to start with the simplest thing to ensure that wireless connectivity works physically before you start changing software settings in your PC and router. But you need to work towards the best settings you can get on your router.

In summary, your wireless credentials are likely to include:

- SSID of the router

- Encryption protocol (examples: WEP, WPA, WPA2)

- Encryption cypher (examples: TKIP, AES)

- Shared secret, or pre-shared key, a 'passphrase' you choose to limit access to your wireless network

- MAC address of the wireless card on your PC. To obtain this, go to **Start->Run**, enter 'cmd.exe /k ipconfig /all' to display all your network adaptors and look for the Physical Address of the network adaptor with 'Wireless' in its name. The MAC address will look similar to '00-0C-41-AF-9C-92'.

When you've established what credentials you need, make sure you've noted them somewhere you can find them easily and other people can't.

Action 1

Go to **Control Panel->Network Connections** on XP (In Vista it's **Control Panel->Network and Sharing Center** and then select **Manage Network Connections**) and see what network connections are available. If you have a LAN or high-speed Internet connection with **Connected** in the **Status** column, and you still can't connect to the Internet, you probably have a router problem.

Action 2

If you have a router connection to the Internet, locate any documentation you have for the router (remember some might be on a CD). Find out how to run its web interface to display the line state, and what any lights on the front mean. You may need to provide your service credentials on one of the router pages. Routers can be confusing, so try not to change things at random. Make notes of anything you do change. If the telephone line (sometimes called 'WAN connection') state as seen by the router is inactive or disconnected, and remains so for some time, contact your service provider.

Action 3

If you have a dial-up network adaptor listed, try right-clicking on the adaptor in **Network Connections** and selecting **Connect** from the pop-up menu. You will be asked for your service credentials, then the modem will try to make a call to the number listed. 'No dial tone' means you have a cable problem (see Connections, Chapter Three, Section 1). In the event of other problems, check your credentials and the phone number you're calling.

Action 4

If you have a wireless network adaptor listed, first ensure it's enabled. Right-click and select **Enable** if it isn't. Then right-click and select **Properties** from the pop-up menu (see Fig 21 or Fig. 22 for Vista).Under the **Wireless Networks** tab, you need to **Add** a preferred network for your wireless LAN using your wireless

credentials. Alternatively, if your wireless LAN's SSID
name appears when you right-click the adaptor and select
View Available Wireless Networks, you can select your
network and click **Connect**. Remember, your network
won't appear in the list if you have SSID broadcast turned
off in your wireless router or access point.

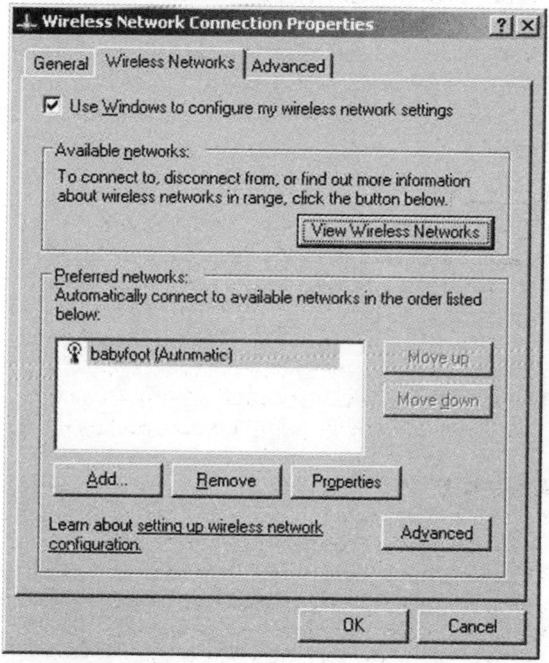

Fig. 21

```
┌─────────────────────────────────────────────────────┐
│ BeBox Wireless Network properties              [ ⌧ ] │
│ ┌──────────┬──────────┐                              │
│ │Connection│ Security │                              │
│ │          └──────────┴────────────────────────────┐ │
│ │                                                  │ │
│ │  Name:             BeBox                         │ │
│ │  SSID:             BeBox                         │ │
│ │  Network Type:     Access point                  │ │
│ │  Network Availability:  All users                │ │
│ │                                                  │ │
│ │  ☑ Connect automatically when this network is in range │
│ │  ☑ Connect to a more preferred network if available │
│ │  ☐ Connect even if the network is not broadcasting │
│ │                                                  │ │
│ │                                                  │ │
│ └──────────────────────────────────────────────────┘ │
│                                    ┌──────┐ ┌──────┐ │
│                                    │  OK  │ │Cancel│ │
│                                    └──────┘ └──────┘ │
└─────────────────────────────────────────────────────┘
```

Fig. 22

Web browsing

If your browser doesn't work on any web page, you probably have a connection problem. If it works on some but not others, maybe you're seeing some broken pages, but probably the page wants to use facilities in your browser that you turned off for security reasons. You need to decide whether you trust the site enough to give it access to your facilities.

When the text on web pages is too big or too small, you can usually adjust it if you look under the View menu.

LAN browsing

If you have more than one PC on your LAN you can easily set them to join a workgroup with a name chosen by you and share files with each other. You will then be able to browse the disk and printer resources of other PCs in the workgroup. See 'I want to share some files' in Section 2 of this chapter for further details. To use shared printers, open **Control Panel->Printers And Faxes**. Click the **Add Printer** icon and the **Add Printer Wizard** will appear. Select '**A network printer, or a printer attached to another computer**', and the wizard will scan your LAN looking for printers you can use. If printers you expect don't appear, check they're actually turned on and connected to the LAN.

Section 4:
Email and communication

Email is one of the most widely used applications worldwide. Its unparalleled ability to allow people to communicate quickly, regardless of distance and time zones, has made email a fundamental part of most businesses and many people's everyday lives.

Of course, as it is so widely used, it is also one of the greatest sources of frustration. Not so much due to problems with software, but more due to the sheer amount of it you receive. Like a telephone ringing, most people just have to read and possibly answer an email when it arrives, and many find that they seem to spend their whole day dealing with email. Businesses now lose so much constructive work time to staff dealing with email that an industry has sprung up devoted to training people how to do it.

By far the most annoying and time-consuming aspect of email is spam. Spam can be loosely defined as any email you don't want and didn't ask for. Usually it consists of advertising, chain letters and scams originating from some unknown server somewhere in the world, but it may come from people you know, with or without their knowledge. Contrary to the Monty Python song that email spam is named after, it is neither lovely nor wonderful, nor is it perpetrated for the most part by Vikings.

Note: in the following examples we assume you are using Microsoft Outlook or Outlook Express. If you would like to try an alternative email client, we recommend you try something like Thunderbird (see Useful Resources).

EXPERT TIP

In the course of your Internet career, you will probably change your service provider at least once. When you do, all of a sudden you will not be able to send or receive email via me@myoldprovider.com, so you have to contact everyone you expect to email you explaining your address change. We think that's inconvenient and largely unnecessary.

For about £5 a year, you can buy an Internet domain name like www.mydomain.com and this will give you an email address at me@mydomain.com. Now you can set it up to automatically redirect all mail sent to

---

me@myoldprovider.com. When you change providers, all you have to do is change the redirect to point to me@ mynewprovider.com, and you don't have to worry about people not being able to contact you any more – as far as they're concerned you're still at me@mydomain.com.

I'm getting loads of spam

Tell us about it. At the time of writing, it is estimated that there are a mind-boggling 100 billion spam emails sent every day. If every man, woman and child on the planet had a computer, that would come to around 15 each. If you only get 15 a day you should consider yourself lucky.

What can be done about it? Not a lot. Despite the fact that sending spam is illegal in many countries, it's still on the increase. All you can really do is configure your PC to get rid of it the best it can.

Action 1

Almost all email providers (Yahoo, Google, Hotmail, your Internet service provider, etc.) provide some sort of spam filtering facility. Check your email configuration online to make sure you're using it. Most can be set to delete spam automatically or at least move it into a junk folder. The second option is probably better, because email filters aren't perfect and may well classify something you want as spam. With a junk folder, you can periodically check and make sure there's nothing there you want before binning the rest.

Action 2

Almost all email clients (Outlook, Thunderbird etc.) also have a spam filter. Make sure it's turned on. Again, it's best to move spam to a junk folder for later checking.

Action 3

Many email clients allow you to set up rules to apply to incoming emails. A good one is to move anything which is sent by someone not in your email address book to the junk folder.

Action 4

Spam filters, online with your email provider or on your PC in your email client, are clever. They learn. So when you see something in your inbox that's spam, click on the **Spam** or **Junk** button so your filter can learn. And if you're reviewing your junk folder and see something that's not spam, click on the **Not Spam** or **Not Junk** button.

Action 5

If you have auto-responding turned on in your email client, turn it off, or at least make sure it checks with you first.

Action 6

Just following the above tips should cut your spam down to the point where it's manageable. However, if you're still finding it too much, consider researching anti-spam software you can install on your PC.

Action 7

Use throwaway email addresses. If you base your email round a domain you control, you can probably set up as many email addresses as you like, whitelisting and blacklisting them as you choose. If you give a different email address at your domain to everyone who asks, when one of them becomes a problem due to spam, it can be simply blacklisted.

EXPERT TIP

Never EVER reply to a spam email. Spam is sent to billions of email addresses, most of which don't exist. If you reply, you're only telling them that your address does exist, so they can send you more, not to mention selling your address to other spammers as well. 'Click here to remove yourself from this mailing list' is an invitation to treat with extreme caution in anything you think may be a spam email.

I can't receive any emails

If you're not receiving any emails, it could be due to one of several causes.

Action 1

Make sure your email software is connecting properly. Is there an error message like 'server too busy' or 'invalid password'? If so, then you may just have to wait or check your account settings. Can you send yourself an email? If so, then the problem is more likely to be at your email provider's end. Is your software configured correctly? Double-check on your provider's website – most have a guide to the setting you should have in your email client.

Action 2
Use your browser to log on to the web mail interface for your email service. Do you have any email to receive? Maybe you're just not very popular. Is your inbox full? Many accounts have a limit on the amount of space your email can use, so you may have to delete some old ones. Is your account suspended? Check with your provider if it looks like they've turned you off for some reason. Has your subscription to the service expired?

Action 3
Check the junk folder in your client and with your online provider. Is it moving everything you receive to junk? Maybe the spam filter settings are too restrictive and you need to adjust them.

Action 4
If all these things fail to turn up results, you may need to contact your service provider to see if there's any problem at their end. Some of their software may be broken, or there may be a problem with your account they were unaware of.

I can't send any emails
There are two possibilities here; you're trying to send emails for the first time and they won't work, or you've

been happily sending them for a while and all of a sudden sending stops working.

Action 1

First ensure you're not getting any obvious error messages when sending the email, that you've got a valid email address in the address box and that your provider's server is active and working (you can check their website for this information).

Action 2

If you're setting up your client for the first time and it won't send emails, you've probably got the configuration wrong. Check your account settings on the client. To do this click on **Tools-> Accounts-> Other Properties**, then select your email account in the list and press the **Properties** button (see Figs. 23, 24 and 25). Most clients like Outlook have a facility to send a test email. Try it – did it work? If so, then the problem's not with your connection. Is the outgoing mail server correct? Some providers use quite different names for the incoming and outgoing mail servers. Is your user ID correct? Some providers have an account ID, like jqsmith, while others use an email address, like john.smith@provider.com. Is the password correct? Try typing it in again, making sure you get the upper and lower case letters in the right case. Also, check any SMTP settings your provider may require (see next action). Do you need a user ID and password at all? If you're connected by a cable modem or ADSL line, you may not need them, and providing them can confuse the poor dumb machine on the other end.

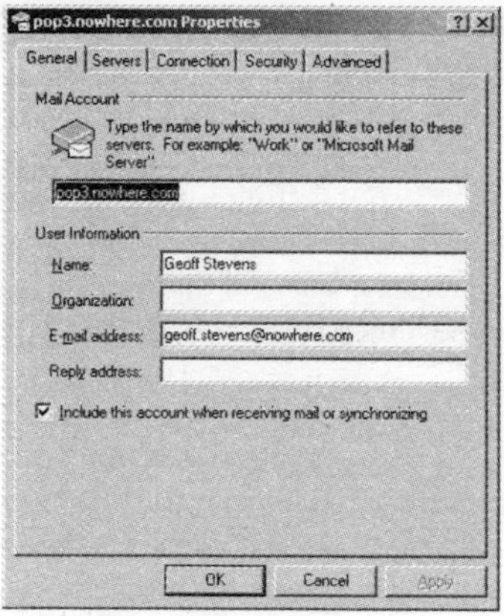
pop3.nowhere.com Properties
General
Servers
Connection
Security
Advanced
Mail Account
Type the name by which you would like to refer to these servers. For example: "Work" or "Microsoft Mail Server".
pop3.nowhere.com
User Information
Name:
Geoff Stevens
Organization:
E-mail address:
geoff.stevens@nowhere.com
Reply address:
Include this account when receiving mail or synchronizing
OK
Cancel
Apply

Fig. 23

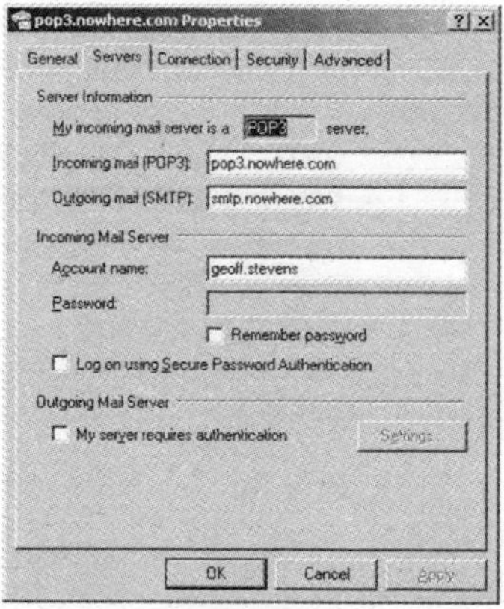
pop3.nowhere.com Properties
General
Servers
Connection
Security
Advanced
Server Information
My incoming mail server is a POP3 server.
Incoming mail (POP3):
pop3.nowhere.com
Outgoing mail (SMTP):
smtp.nowhere.com
Incoming Mail Server
Account name:
geoff.stevens
Password:
Remember password
Log on using Secure Password Authentication
Outgoing Mail Server
My server requires authentication
Settings...
OK
Cancel
Apply

Fig. 24

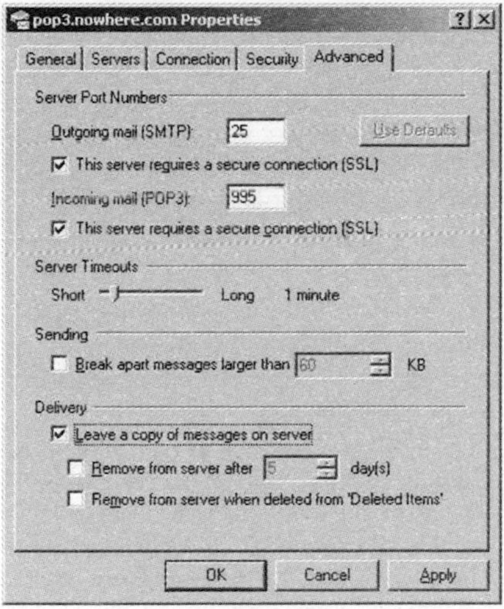

Fig. 25

Action 3

If your email has been sending OK for a while, and then suddenly stops, the most probable cause is that your email provider has introduced SMTP authorisation. This is a secure way of checking that the person sending the email is who they say they are, and is used by most providers now, and probably by all providers in the near future. If your provider has changed, they should have sent you an email about it, but if not you can find the information on their website, probably in the support section under 'configuration'. Make sure you check the password and

ID settings are correct, and if your client allows it, the port number to connect on.

Action 4

If all else fails, do you have another outgoing mail server you can try? If you have more than one email provider (and many people do for multiple email addresses). Try sending through the other server. If that works, contact the support section of the provider that's failing to send – the problem is likely to be at their end.

SMTP, POP AND IMAP

Like the real mail service, where you post a letter in a letterbox, but receive letters from the postman, emails you send don't go by the same channel as those you receive. When you send an email, it's sent to the Simple Mail Transfer Protocol (SMTP) server of your email service provider. When you receive email, it's delivered by a Post Office Protocol (POP) or Internet Message Access Protocol (IMAP) server. Any or all of these servers may require a user ID and password, so when you're setting up an email account in your mail client, make sure you have the details of the server names, any user IDs and passwords needed, and which protocol (IMAP or POP) to use for email delivery.

I am sending an email but it's stuck in the outbox

Sometimes when a message is very large, or sent to a lot of people, or there's a bad connection to the server, an email will be sent but remain in your outbox. Then the next time you send mail it gets sent again, and again, and eventually you get a message from the recipient saying 'Why are you spamming me?'

Action 1

Delete the message from your outbox manually. This may seem obvious, but many people don't think of it. The disadvantage with this fix is that it won't necessarily stop it happening again.

Action 2

Check your anti-virus software configuration for the area involving outgoing emails and attachments. If you think this might be responsible, just turn your anti-virus software off for a moment, try sending the email again, and then turn the anti-virus back on. If the email was sent and disappeared from your inbox, then the anti-virus software is responsible for the problem. Check the documentation or the manufacturer's online support for possible solutions.

Action 3

It may be that your email software has a corruption in the file it uses to store your email. If you think this is the problem, back up your data, then delete the email data files. Check on your software manufacturer's website or Google for how to do this for your client. Restart your client (you'll have to reconfigure it from scratch) and see if this fixes the problem. If it does, you can try importing your old email from the backup you made at the start.

I sent an email but it didn't save a copy on my PC

Most email is set up to automatically save an email to a 'Sent Items' folder. Check your email client's options and preferences. If you're not saving emails after sending, it's 99 per cent likely that this setting is turned off.

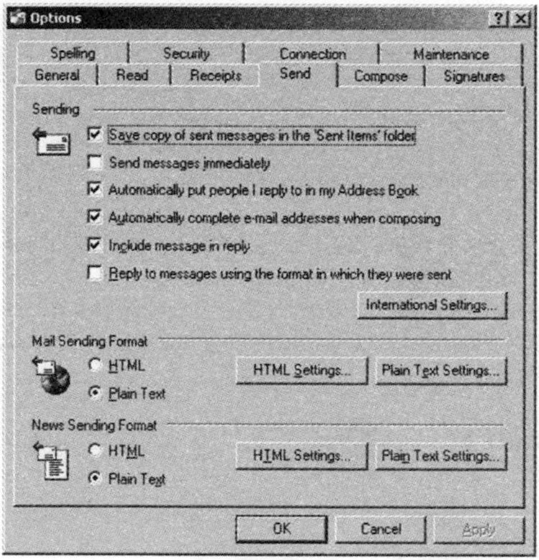

Fig. 26

I sent someone an email and it never arrived

This could be one of two problems: you're not sending it, or they're not receiving it.

Action 1

Try sending a different email to the same person. If they receive that, then there's a problem with the email itself. Maybe it's the wrong address. Check for any error messages when you send the problem email, and review the 'I can't send any email' section above.

Action 2

Try sending an email to someone else. If you can't send it to anyone, review the 'I can't send any email' section. If it's just the one person that has the problem, then they should check their spam filter. Maybe it's in the junk folder. Or maybe they're not getting any email and they need to resolve that problem.

Action 3

If the email is very large, maybe it was too big for the recipient's inbox. Get them to check their settings and see if their inbox is full.

Action 4

It is possible that a very large email or one sent to many recipients has been flagged as spam by someone en route. If there are a lot of recipients, try sending it to just one.

Check with your service provider and get the recipient to do the same. It may be that the service provider has decided it's spam or it was reported as spam to them. We had a problem once where BT itself was flagged as a spammer by one of the services that detect spam flying around the Internet and got on an email blacklist. It took a day or two to get off again.

Action 5
Check your inbox for 'Undelivered Mail Returned To Sender' type messages. While these messages are written by machines for techies to read, they usually contain valuable clues about why mail isn't delivered. The message may say it's never heard of the recipient, in which case you may have mistyped the email address. Or it may say the recipient's mailbox is full.

Someone sent me an email and it never arrived
This is just the reverse of the section above. Try the same things, but reverse the sender and recipient roles.

I can't open an attachment
The best way to open any attachment is to right-click on it, save it to your file system, virus scan the saved file and then open the saved file as you would normally. This can save you a lot of grief in the long run. However, if you want to just double-click on the attachment, read on.

Action 1

Outlook (and some other clients) automatically stop you from opening an attachment because they view the file as a security risk. If you're absolutely sure you want to open it, go to **Tools->Options->Security** and uncheck the option that says do not open potentially dangerous files (see Fig. 27). On your own head be it.

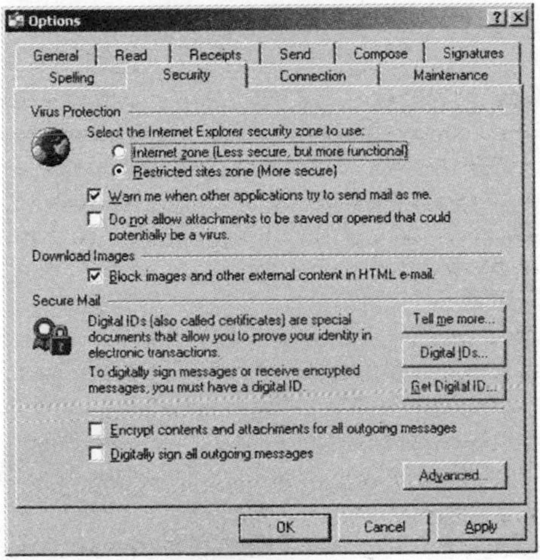

Fig. 27

Action 2

If that doesn't work, ask the person who sent it to compress it with WinZip or WinRar and resend it. You can then extract it from the compressed file and open it. Another method would be for them to rename it as whatever.txt. Save it when it arrives, and rename it back to the proper extension.

I can't see pictures in an email

This problem could be due to email client security settings, the format of the email, the format you view emails in, or even problems with the picture itself (just because it claims to be a jpeg doesn't mean it is).

Action 1

If it's just one particular picture or email you want to see pictures in, you can usually right-click on the picture and select a 'display picture' option. Or there may be a button which will show all pictures in an email.

Action 2

Most email clients will not show pictures by default unless they're from a trusted source. Trusted sources in this case are generally considered to be people in your address book. If you get emails from someone like your bank and would rather have the pictures displayed automatically, add them to your address book.

Action 3

Most clients also have various options for controlling the display of pictures. Look for security settings in your application options and review them to display pictures according to your personal preferences.

Action 4

If you are viewing the email in plain text mode, pictures won't be displayed but will be present as attachments. You can open the attachment, or change your view options (there's usually an option on a **View** menu, or a setting in **Options->Read**).

Action 5

Ask the person who sent it if they're sure the picture was actually sent. Many clients have options which suppress sending of pictures.

Action 6

If all else fails, check the picture is really a picture by right-clicking on it, saving it to your disk and then opening it with your image viewing software.

Hyperlinks in messages aren't working

On the whole, this is a good thing. Clicking on a link in an email message is fraught with peril. You don't really know where it's going to take you, whether it will install anything nasty on your machine. Having said that, you will get real, useful links from people you know and organisations you deal with.

Action 1

We recommend not clicking on the links in the first place. If you open your browser and copy and paste the link address into the address box, at least you know you're going where the link says you are. If the email claims to be from your bank or another organisation, you're probably better off going to their real website and looking for the information from there.

Action 2

OK, so you want to be able to click those links anyway. Usually they should work by default, but if they don't check the options for your client. Many have an option to disable links, and this may be switched on.

Action 3

If they still don't work, check that you have a default web browser set up by going to **Start->Control Panel->Add or Remove Programs** (see Fig. 28). If you don't have a default browser, no links will work as Windows doesn't know what browser to pass them to.

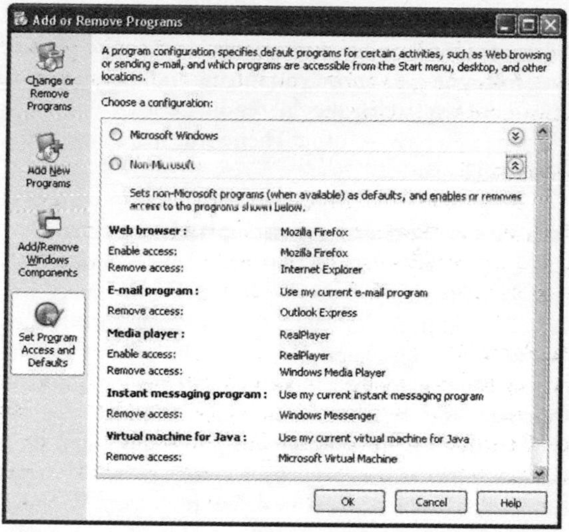

Fig. 28

Action 4

You might try going to Windows Explorer and finding the file-type associations you have set up (see 'The file is opening in the wrong application', Section 2 of this chapter). Make sure the URL file type is set up to open in your preferred browser.

I think my email has a virus

Delete it. Don't mess around, just delete it. If it came from someone you know, you might send them an email out of courtesy saying they're sending out viruses – they probably aren't aware of it. Then virus scan your whole PC just to be sure.

I've received an email chain letter

Almost all email chain letters are scams. Some aren't. There's a famous one about a boy dying of cancer who wanted to get in the *Guinness Book of Records* for the most get well cards. The good news is he did get in the book, having accumulated 33 million cards in two years, and the better news is he recovered from cancer and is now healthy. The bad news is he's still getting cards and is fed up to the back teeth with it. So even if there's a remote chance the email is genuine, best to delete it anyway. Whatever you do, don't send it on. As with snail mail chain letters, electronic ones are illegal.

Action 1

The best thing to do when you get anything you think has even the slightest chance of being a scam of some sort is to go to www.snopes.com and search their database. Snopes is a first-class source of information about urban legend, email scams and the like. If we find something there that says it is a scam and we know the person who sent it, we like to email them back with a link to the Snopes article and say they should check these things before adding to the problem. If they don't learn from that, they probably won't send you one again out of embarrassment if nothing else.

My email messages mysteriously disappear

Make sure you're looking in the right place – your emails might be getting routed to a folder apart from your inbox, or you may have your inbox sorted by something other than date.

If it's not the obvious things, it may have happened because Outlook was compacting its database and was interrupted, or its database was somehow corrupted. It's a good idea to make sure you're working offline when compacting Outlook folders (see below). This can be a very serious error, and the chances are you may not be able to recover your old emails.

If your old emails are very important, you should regularly back up the data files. You can find out where these are by looking in **Options->Tools** and clicking on the **Maintenance** tab (in Vista: **Tools->Options ->Advanced**). Or you can regularly export your data to another file (**File->Export**).

Action 1

If you suspect Outlook data file corruption, the best thing to do is to immediately shut down Outlook, back up the data files, then restart Outlook and compact all your folders immediately. If this doesn't help, Microsoft has an inbox repair kit tool which may sort things out. You can find full details and instructions for this on the Microsoft website.

Action 2

If all else fails, you can delete the Outlook data files, restart Outlook and start from scratch.

I can't delete an email

If you can't delete an email, or Outlook locks out when you click on the email, it's likely that it contains a virus.

Action 1

Check that your email client is up to date. Some older clients activate viruses when previewing them. Check that your anti-virus software is up to date as well, and that it is configured to check your email.

Action 2

Turn off the Outlook preview pane and try to delete the message.

Action 3

Try holding down the **Shift** key while you press **Delete**. This deletes the message without putting it in the **Deleted Items** folder.

How can I stop Outlook Express compacting my folders?

This one's easy to fix. There's an option in Outlook Express (**Options->Tools->Maintenance** tab, or in Vista, **Tools->Options->Advanced**) which you can set to compact your email data periodically. This is done to save space, but can take some time and must not be interrupted. If you want to change how often this occurs, or set it so it only happens when you specifically ask it to compact the database, make the appropriate changes to these settings.

I can't hear the other caller in my VOIP application / The other caller can't hear me

---

EXPERT TIP

Most VOIP services have a test call facility. This allows you to make a test call, leave a brief message, and then listen while the message is played back to you. In Skype, you can do this by placing a call to Echo123. For all VOIP problems this is a good starting place to check things are working. If you can hear the call and the message plays back OK, then the set up on your PC is OK and the problem lies with the other caller, or maybe with the Internet itself.

Problems with one caller not being able to hear another usually stem from a problem with one, if not both, of the callers' set-ups. It's a good idea for both callers to go through these steps to see where the problem lies.

Action 1

Make a test call (see the expert tip above). This should narrow the problem down by identifying who has the real problem.

Action 2

Check the headphone and microphone leads are plugged in correctly. Make sure they're plugged into the right sockets and not swapped with each other. Make sure the volume on your headphones is not way down, and that the speakers aren't muted in Windows. You can test the headphones by playing some music, and the microphone can be tested via **Start->Control Panel->Sounds and Audio Devices**.

Action 3

Check in the documentation for your hardware (headset, USB phone etc.) to see if it needs some specific driver software or application running, and if so check this is installed and working.

Action 4

Check in your VOIP application's **Options** or **Preferences**. Are all the devices assigned to the right headphones and microphone? Is there any facility for testing the audio components?

My VOIP sound quality is poor

The most common cause for this is a poor connection to the Internet. You should check all the cables and plugs are inserted correctly and look in good shape first, and if you bought a very cheap headset or phone, well, you get what you pay for. But assuming that's all OK, the odds are that there is just not enough bandwidth on your Internet connection to give you good quality.

Action 1

Check to see if you, or someone else on your local network, is downloading any large files. If they're hogging all the bandwidth, you will have to wait for them to finish.

Action 2

If you're on a dial-up connection, then tough. We're sort of amazed you could place the call in the first place. Dial-up connections just aren't fast enough.

Action 3

If you've got an active webcam, turn it off. Video takes a lot more bandwidth than just sound.

I keep getting messages from people I don't know on my instant messenger

A common enough problem. As soon as you sign up for MSNLive Messenger (or any other instant messaging product), you advertise your existence to everyone and his dog.

Action 1

Set up privacy for your instant messenger. In Live Messenger, it's **Tools->Options->Privacy**. You should see some option along the lines of 'only allow people in my contact/allow list to contact me'. Check this option and you'll stop getting those unsolicited messages.

Section 5:
Applications

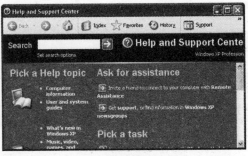

Fig. 29

Most of the problems you will experience on a day-to-day basis will be software problems. Hardware problems tend to be much rarer and often catastrophic in nature, but software problems will crop up frequently. The good news is that most software problems are easily resolved; usually it's just a matter of changing a preference or an option and everything is fine again. The bad news is that it can be difficult to find out which option to tweak and what to change it to. Frustration and the feeling that the program is more user-mendacious than user-friendly can mount rapidly. Whatever else you do, we recommend that you don't give in to the urge to put a brick through your screen. Despite the temporary feeling of satisfaction such actions generate, it rarely helps in the long run.

There's a universe of software applications out there, from abacus simulators to Zen koan generators. Some of them are even useful. To list common problems and solutions for all of them would be impossible. In the earlier sections of this chapter, we've covered the stuff most people have – an operating system, email, browsing, networking and the file system. All the other applications you run – word processors, spreadsheets, databases, games, imaging software, media players and so on are somewhat idiosyncratic, because they all do different things. It would probably take a book this size just to list all the applications commonly used, let alone common problems for all of them.

YOUR PERSONAL COMPUTER

Almost everybody uses their PC for web browsing and communications like email and instant messaging. Most people use several other applications, stuff that makes their PC useful and interesting for them – for example, applications for word processing, photograph organisation and music collecting. The particular set of applications you run on your computer is what makes it personal.

Most of the available applications we've probably never or barely heard of, much less used ourselves. But, and this is a big but, we're still among the first people friends, family and work colleagues turn to when they have problems. Why? Sadly, it's not because we're geniuses. Or even if we are, that's not why they ask us. It's because we know HOW to solve problems. How to investigate the problem, how to narrow down possible causes, and where to look for help and solutions.

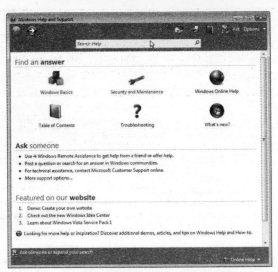

Fig. 30

DOWN THE RABBIT HOLE TO WONDERLAND

When we're researching a technical problem, we sometimes say we're 'stuck down a rabbit hole'. There comes a point where you need to make a judgement between spending another few hours testing possible solutions to whatever technical problem you're dealing with, and getting out of the rabbit hole for a while to see whether there's a better approach.

Would another application do the job of the one you're having a problem with? Is there another way to do what you want to do that avoids the problem you're having? If you've invested some time and you can't see an end to it yet, stepping back to re-examine the problem can reap rewards.

> Another risk when you're down the rabbit hole is promises of solutions 'in the next release'. While many such promises are made in good faith, they're not always delivered. Following them can truly lead you to Wonderland. We never make buying decisions based on promises of features that 'will be delivered'.

So, you've got some specific problem with an application? Do what we do. Approach the problem logically. Eliminate possible causes. Look for clues. Look for answers in documentation or online. Ask questions of others. Try things out. Don't forget to curse and swear a lot.

All these general problem-solving techniques are covered in much greater detail in Chapter 2. Read that chapter and work through the problem as you go, and you should be able to find the solution to almost any problem.

However, for those of you who prefer to read the digest version and figure out the rest yourself, here are the most important things you can do when solving a problem:

● **Learn about the software**

A lot of these problems can be avoided by learning what your applications can do, what features they have, and what options and preferences can be set for them. Most people tend to just turn on the computer, open up the application and charge ahead full speed. As many applications look and behave a lot like each other, you can be pretty productive this way, but when something goes wrong you can be left floundering without a clue where to start. And you can also spend a great deal of time doing something which the application will actually do for you with just a click or two.

In a way it's a lot like driving. You can get into a new car and look around and identify the gear stick, the pedals, the handbrake, lights and windscreen wipers and then put your foot down and drive off. However, when you're stranded on the side of the M1 waiting two hours for the AA to arrive, you begin to wish you'd found out where to check the oil levels before setting off.

● **Read the manual**

Luckily both cars and software have a good place to start finding out things. It's called the manual. In a car you'll usually find it in the glove compartment. In an application, it's usually found by clicking on **Help** on the menu bar at the top of the application, and then selecting **MyApplication Help** (or something similar).

Unluckily, software designers are no better, and often worse, than car companies in laying out the manual in a comprehensible manner, and both fail when it comes to making the manual an interesting read. If you reach the end of the first section and are still awake you're doing well.

Have a look at the table of contents. If there's an introduction section, that's a good place to get familiar with the product in general. If there's a list of features, then that's a good place to find out what sort of things the application is capable of doing. These are both worth reviewing, if not reading in detail, but unless you're especially masochistic we would not recommend sitting down and reading the entire manual from start to end.

Most manuals also have an index, which is sort of useful, and a **Find** facility, which is invaluable. If you're trying to find out something specific, just go to the **Find** tab and type in a few relevant words. It will search the whole manual for those words and present you with a list of possible topics to look at.

● **Use the Internet**

If you can't find what you're looking for in the manual, then try Google. Type in something in more or less plain English (like 'How do I set the background colour to red in Word for Windows' and you'll almost certainly get loads of pages to check for a solution. Forums dedicated to a product, often linked from or part of a manufacturer's website, are also good places to post questions. However, if you're asking in a forum, always use the search facilities in the forum first to see if someone else has asked the same question previously. People helping out in these forums tend to be annoyed by people who ask a question that's been raised a hundred times before.

Chapter Five:
Malware Problems

Malware (malicious software) is software installed on your PC that is designed to exploit you for somebody else's benefit. It's usually described in a long list of categories. We're sorry to tell you lots of clever people are hard at work inventing new ways of getting that malware installed on your PC, so there might be another couple of categories by the time you read this. Whatever the type of malware, once it's installed itself on your PC, that PC is compromised, and you have a malware problem.

What is the malware problem?

We'll start by dividing the consequences of malware problems into three issues: privacy, security and misuse.

- Privacy is your ability to carry out your business without someone looking over your shoulder. You'd think it odd if you visited one bookseller and, as you left, a publisher sent a private detective after you to see what other bookshops you visited. But that kind of tracking can be done with ease on the public Internet and many people even claim it's good for you.

- Security is your ability to protect your assets. Information you type into your computer can be misused to steal property. Like burgling your house, malware that compromises your PC's security is illegal in most territories, but when your PC is connected to nearly every other computer in the world you might expect a few of them to try and have a go.

● Misuse is the issue of whether you're the sole arbiter of what your PC does. It's not hard for a Microsoft Windows PC to be remotely controlled by someone else, making the PC a 'zombie' in a network of compromised machines, or which displays advertising from people you'd never want to hear from without your say-so. Increasingly, PC users are being unwittingly enlisted for even shadier activities than relaying spam (see Security, Section 3, Chapter One). Since you're at least nominally responsible for what goes up and down the cable to your house, or the signal to your phone, if you let such activities continue you may have some explaining to do one day.

Malware, therefore, is anything that makes you consider these issues because software on your PC is behaving badly for somebody else's benefit.

Where does malware come from?

You have to assume your Microsoft Windows installation CD is free of malware (unless you've installed a pirate copy, in which case you probably deserve what you get), and that a newly-installed Windows PC without a network connection is uncompromised. After that, you're pretty much on your own.

● Almost anything you download or install onto your PC may be malware, or contain malware, or under certain circumstances attract malware. Even mainstream applications from respected vendors may contain defects which permit malware to install itself on your PC.

- Web pages you visit, even pages on sites you trust, may compromise your PC by exploiting defects in your web browser. Or web pages may simply convince you to download and install malware. Click here to install malware!

- Emails containing apparently attractive offers will attempt to lure you to toxic websites, or send you booby-trapped media or programs.

EXPERT TIP

When you visit a web page and you see one of those flashing boxes saying something like 'Your PC is infected! Click here to fix it', clicking there will almost certainly install something nasty. Just say no.

If this is starting to sound scary, that's because it *is* scary. Those clever malware writers are making huge sums of money from their activities and they're unlikely to stop refining their methods. But, like the two hikers being chased by a bear, you don't have to run faster than the bear to escape. You just have to run faster than the other hiker. There's a huge number of easily-compromised computers connected to the Internet. Following some simple measures can reduce your chances of malware infestation considerably, by making your PC harder to compromise than thousands of others.

GUNFIGHT AT THE INTERNET CORRAL

While there are a lot of people trying to put malware on your PC, luckily there are lots of other talented people who are working just as hard to identify the malware compromises and exploits. They put a stop to them by sharing the information they uncover about malware and providing solutions to computer users. The struggle between the two sides has been likened to an arms race, with each side deploying ever-more-sophisticated weapons.

In the computer security industry, the people involved on each side of this shootout are identified like cowboys in an old Western film, by the colour of the hats they wear. The baddies, eager to rustle a herd of PCs for their own gain, are called 'black hat hackers', and those who fight for fairness and justice are the 'white hat hackers'. 'Hacker' is just a general term for a technically-advanced software developer.

Like the movies, it's not unknown for people to change sides. Some 'white hats' used to be 'black hats'. In the morally ambiguous world in which we live there are also 'grey hats'. These are people who seem to know a lot about the subject, but their motivation is unclear. They might be on a journey between the two sides.

What types of malware are there?

Here's a list of some of the ways inventive black hats have found to compromise your PC, so far.

- Cookies. These are usually a perfectly normal part of web browsing. However, there are reasons to be concerned about 'third party' or 'tracking' cookies, used by advertising networks to track the browser at every site using the network. They can compile long-term browsing histories which can compromise your privacy.

● Adware is commercial software which shows you unsolicited advertisements, usually in pop-up windows or browser windows that open themselves. Your PC is being misused.

● Spyware is commercial software that silently leaks information about your browsing habits to a third party. Like tracking cookies, this can compromise your privacy.

● Browser hijackers change the settings of your browser without your knowledge or consent, taking you to sites which are usually full of pay-per-click advertising. Your home page may be altered and you may be unable to change the settings back. This is misusing your PC and the altered browser settings may compromise your security.

● Affiliate fee grabbers snatch the money that can be made on the Internet by receiving affiliate fees when a web page refers a browser to another site, such as Dell or Amazon. The affiliate fee grabber waits until you visit such a site, then supplies the black hat's affiliate code to claim the fee. Your PC is being misused.

● Diallers generate revenue by making a PC with a modem connect to the Internet via a premium rate number. They may change the default Internet connection settings and make calls at their own discretion. Your security is compromised, because you will pick up the phone bill. These scams have become less popular with the rise of broadband access.

● Back doors and trojans permit remote operation of your PC. Black hats can use your connection to launch scams and attacks against other Internet users, as well as sniffing what you type and viewing what's on your screen. This is misuse and also compromises your privacy and security.

● Root kits are back doors which deploy advanced techniques to make themselves hard to find. They subvert the operating system's tools to make themselves invisible to anything other than detailed inspection.

● Viruses and worms spread from computer to computer automatically, usually carrying a payload program that eventually damages infected systems. The damage can vary from simply displaying a message to making the PC un-bootable. Viruses have become less of a problem in the twenty-first century, as it's hard to make money out of just damaging computers. There was a brief vogue for viruses which encrypted files on your PC, then demanded ransom payments to un-encrypt them, but this is a difficult way to make money compared to stealing credit card details from your browser.

Section 1:
How do I know if my PC
has malware installed?

Luckily, a lot of malware makes itself obvious, because its payoff comes from showing you advertisements, and it needs your PC's resources to do that. Some symptoms often seen with malware problems are:

- You experience poor performance, especially while on the Internet.

- Your PC stops responding for extended periods with increasing frequency.

- Start-up times when you turn your computer on become longer.

- Your web browser closes unexpectedly, or stops responding.

- Performing a search from an engine like Google produces results from a different site from the one you started on.

- Clicking on a link does nothing, or takes you to an apparently unrelated website.

- Your browser's home page changes to a different site and you can't reset it.

- Extra toolbars appear in your browser when you didn't ask for them.

- Web pages are automatically added to your favourites.

- Your browser's security settings change without your knowledge.

- Pop-up advertising windows appear when your browser isn't running, or over web pages you wouldn't expect to display pop-ups, or whole browser windows open with advertising unexpectedly.

- Desktop icons appear when you don't expect them.

- Parts of Windows or other programs stop working.

If you have more than four of these symptoms (or even one if it's advertisements popping up unexpectedly when you're not browsing the Internet), you should definitely investigate the possibility of a malware problem.

Section 2:
What can I do about malware installed on my PC?

If your PC is displaying a lot of the symptoms from the list above, especially the later ones, you might like to take Ripley's advice from the film *Aliens* and 'nuke it from orbit, it's the only way to be sure'. That means booting from the Windows CD, reformatting your disk and doing a complete reinstall. It's certainly what we'd recommend for a PC used for business, or as a server for other PCs. Malware infestations typically start off with some adware or spyware, but once the black hats have a handle on your identity as a compromised PC, they will sell your details on to other black hats who will install further malware, and so on until your PC is groaning under the weight of malware it's running. Once you've reached that stage, clearing up the mess from inside the running PC can be difficult. Because it's hard to be sure that all malware has been removed, we'd start from scratch with a PC used for sensitive data.

I'VE GOT AN ANTI-VIRUS PACKAGE, SO MY PC'S SAFE, RIGHT?

In the gentle days of the late twentieth century, this was largely true. Today, malware mutates with frightening speed. No package has 100 per cent coverage of all the threats on the web. We recommend you deploy several solutions to provide wider coverage.

If you have a malware infestation at an earlier stage, the software solutions we suggest below may be able to clear it up.

Virus malware detection and removal

If you don't have an up-to-date anti-virus package installed, install one immediately. While viruses aren't the leading edge of malware threats these days, there are plenty still in circulation. Virus packages usually update themselves daily with the latest virus details. Some anti-virus packages also claim to detect and remove adware and spyware. Explore these features if your package has them, but be aware they're rarely a complete solution.

We recommend AVG Free Edition (see Useful Resources).

Adware and spyware malware detection and removal

Like anti-virus packages, anti-adware and -spyware packages will update themselves with details of the latest threats.

We recommend you download and install the free versions of Ad-Aware by Lavasoft and Spybot: Search And Destroy (for more on both, see Useful Resources) and follow their very clear instructions on how to run them.

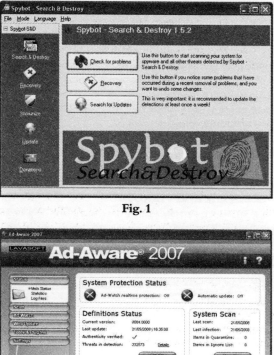

Fig. 1

Fig. 2

Microsoft Windows Defender is another free malware removal tool, but it's been found in tests to fail to detect a large proportion of spyware and adware. However, it may have been improved by the time you read this, and installing and running it is unlikely to do any harm to your PC, so you may want to give it a try. Vista comes with it installed, so all you have to do is make sure it's turned on and set to check for problems regularly (**Control Panel->Windows Defender**).

Other malware detection and removal

What about hijackers, trojans, back doors, root kits, worms and the rest of the list we gave you above? We expect that running anti-virus and one or more anti-spyware packages will cover most instances of these threats. But as we've explained, new threats appear daily. In some cases you may need to research specialised advice.

While running several tools may seem inconvenient, this is currently the safest way to detect as much adware and spyware as possible.

Action 1

Ensure you're running an anti-virus package and it is set to run and update itself automatically.

Action 2

Install more than one anti-spyware package and set them to run automatically.

Action 3

If your problem doesn't improve, seek specialist advice, or reinstall Microsoft Windows.

Section 3:
How can I avoid malware problems?

Removal of malware once it's installed can be difficult or impossible. Clearly, it would better not to have the problem in the first place.

The Internet

Just being connected to the Internet means pretty well anyone in the world might be talking to your PC. If you're using a modem to connect to the Internet, or using a wireless access point you don't control, there is nothing at all between your PC and all the malicious software in the world.

Action 1

Ensure you have a working firewall on your PC. Check in **Control Panel->Security Centre** (see Fig 3). Then click on the **Advanced** tab (see Fig. 4). The default Windows Firewall is certainly better than nothing. A working firewall is absolutely essential if you're using a modem, not a local network, to connect to the Internet, or using a public wireless access point.

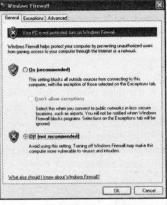

Fig. 3

Fig. 4

Action 2

When using your PC at home, try to use a router and a network cable to your PC. The router will probably provide a valuable extra layer of protection.

Action 3

If you have a wireless router, ensure that you have encryption turned on, using the best encryption your wireless router and PCs can support. Currently this is WPA2. You will probably have to consult your router's documentation to find out how to do this. It's also a good idea to set the router to hide your wireless SSID. If that goes well, set your router to only accept the MAC addresses from PCs you want to use the wireless networks (see Internet and networking, Section 3 of Chapter Four). To access your wireless network security setup go to **Start-> Other Settings-> Network Connections**, then select your wireless network adaptor, right-click to being up **Properties**, select the **Wireless Networks** tab, select the relevant wireless network and click on the **Properties** tab (see Fig. 5)

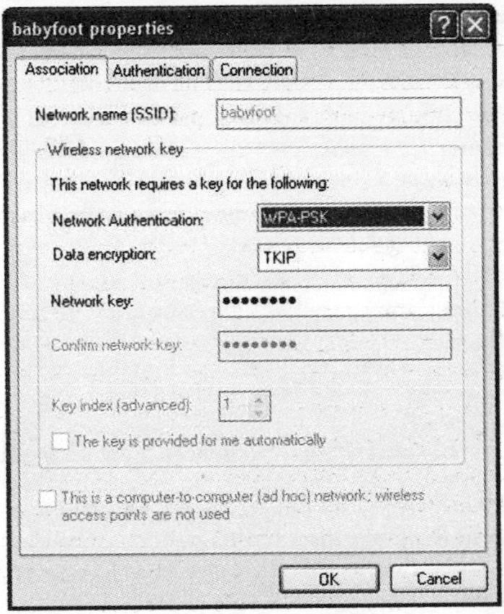

Fig. 5

Action 4

Keep your software up to date. It's not just your browser and email programs which connect to the Internet. Mainstream applications from respected suppliers have suffered from defects making them vulnerable to network exploitation by malware. Applying all available updates reduces the chance of vulnerabilities in code you're running. Most software these days has an option in its **Preferences** or **Options** settings to get the software to check for new updates on a regular basis.

Action 5

If you're running file-sharing software, be careful how you set it up. We've seen examples of people so keen to share their files they've made their whole PC's disk visible to the public Internet. Ensure your file-sharing software is set to operate on only a limited part of your file system.

MALWARE IN YOUR ROUTER?

The router you use to connect to the Internet is just a small computer, preconfigured to do a specific task. Unfortunately, this means some routers may be prone to malware infestation themselves. As we write, only experimental exploitation of such weaknesses has been reported, but the possibility certainly exists.

If you receive any communication from your Internet service provider about vulnerabilities in a router they have supplied you, or hear anything about vulnerabilities in one you bought yourself, take these warnings seriously. You will need to do further research to authenticate the warning, but when you're sure there's a problem, carefully follow whatever steps are available to fix the problem. Malware in your router would leave your PC vulnerable to all sorts of exploitation.

The Web and your browser

Currently, the most effective way for black hats to install malware on your PC is through your browser. Until recently, telling PC users to 'only visit trusted sites' was worthwhile advice, if a little impractical. Today, malware writers are exploiting defects and vulnerabilities in web server software to inject malware right into sites you would think trustworthy, for unsuspecting browsers to download. While the risks are certainly higher if you point your web browser at Russian 'cheap herbal remedy' sites you heard about in an unsolicited email, the risk of encountering malware still exists when you visit the well-known sites of famous names. The famous names get their web server defects fixed eventually, but there are always new pages being added to a site, as well as plenty of new sites for black hats to attack. We think this situation is likely to continue.

SOCIAL ENGINEERING – YOU'LL KICK YOURSELF WHEN YOU FIND OUT

Malware writers deploy a wide variety of technical tricks and little-known computer knowledge to craft programs that look innocent but aren't. But sometimes the easiest way to install malware on a PC is just to ask the PC user to download and install it themselves.

The art of fooling people into doing things in your interest, not theirs, by appearing to be on their side is called 'social engineering' in the world of malware. No technical tricks are necessary to achieve the outcome; all the engineering is in how you appear.

Beware of sites that show you pages or pop-up windows offering software 'to tune your PC' or 'free anti-virus download'.

Think carefully before you download and install any software. Did you go looking for it on a reputable website, or was it just something you clicked on in a search engine results list?

Clicking on links in unsolicited emails can lead you to sites that look very similar to sites you trust, but are put there by black hat malware writers to harvest your details for their own gain.

How has it become possible to automatically download malware over the web? Today, sophisticated websites don't just download text and pictures into your browser, but also 'scripts' (small programs) which run inside your browser. These scripts enable many of the attractive features you see on web pages, such as visual effects and embedded videos. Because the scripts are running inside your browser, they can sometimes do all the things your browser can, including putting files on your local file system, and changing files that are already there. While these features improve your browsing experience, they can also pose a risk. If a malware writer finds a way to inject their own malicious scripts into a website for you to download, then the risk has become a real problem.

Another effective way to channel malware to your browser is through advertising. Anyone can buy advertising on the Web through an advertising network, which will send anyone's content out to many sites. Internet advertising costs are often low. Advertising networks try to screen the content for known malware, but previously unknown malware is becoming available every day, so they have a problem. This problem can get passed on to you. Follow the actions in this section, and do so before you get a malware infestation.

Action 1

Your anti-virus and anti-spyware packages should be set to automatically detect threats where possible. Regularly run a scan if it's not automatic.

Action 2

Find out where the security settings in your browser are, and review them. Be aware that some sites may stop working normally if you turn scripts off entirely or disable cookies. Ideally, find a way to explicitly extend trust to websites as you need to. Depending on your browser and its version, this may not be possible. If the whole Internet is set as a trusted site, you need to set it to be more restrictive.

Action 3

When browsing, think carefully about any files you download. Think doubly carefully about any programs you download and install. And remember to virus scan them after you download them but before you run them.

Action 4

Be aware of the risk of social engineering. You may have found a website that claims to 'diagnose and fix your PC problems' by simply downloading their programs, or to offer you attractive benefits if you register your details. Do some searches to find out what you can about such sites before you place your trust in them.

Action 5

Consider installing another browser. Microsoft Internet Explorer will come by default with your PC, but we think using Mozilla Firefox (see Useful Resources) as well as Internet Explorer can provide significant benefits.

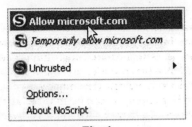

Fig. 6

I'M SECURE, BUT I CAN'T DO ANYTHING!

If you turn security settings up too far on your browser, some websites may stop working properly, because they need to run scripts and use other features of your browser that you've turned off for security reasons. If you install Mozilla Firefox or some other browser, you may also find sites which won't work, insisting on Microsoft Internet Explorer. Frustratingly, these sites can often be your banking or other financial sites. We've found that often you can get a long way into some online payment processes before it becomes apparent you need scripts turned on.

One strategy you can use to get round this is to install Mozilla Firefox and its No-Script plug-in (see Fig. 6). Use Firefox for general browsing with scripts disabled. If you find a site you trust which requires scripts turned on, No-Script makes it easy to temporarily enable a website.

For sites you trust which definitely require scripting or you think might need it because you're making an online payment or purchase, use Microsoft Internet Explorer with security settings permitting you to use the trusted site. Reserve Internet Explorer for sites you really trust, to reduce its exposure to the possibility of malware.

Email and communications

It's estimated that over 75 per cent of the email that flies around the Internet is spam or unsolicited commercial email. Some estimates are much higher. While it's annoying, email that just tries to sell you stuff you don't want is relatively benign (assuming you're not stupid enough to buy into it), as compared to the large amount of spam that tries to lure you to websites designed to steal your personal details, or which tries to get you to install malware programs directly from the email. That spam isn't just unsolicited and commercial, it's positively dangerous. After the Web, email is the black hats' second choice to get their malware running on your PC.

While email makes it easy to share files and URLs, trusting files and URLs from unknown sources is a risky proposition. Even trusted sources like your best friend may be compromised and sending you emails they don't even know they're sending. As you scan your emails, treat with caution any inviting you to click on links, or click on attached files. Is the email from someone you know? Is it a message you might expect to get from that person? Does the attached text sound like the person you expect wrote it? Negative replies to these questions should increase your suspicion of the email.

The same caution should apply to all the communications software you use, such as instant messaging software like Microsoft Messenger or AIM, or voice communications like Skype. Social networking websites like MySpace often offer file-sharing facilities. While the operators of such sites attempt to remove any malware, it's inevitable that some of them will be sources of malware some of the time.

Action 1

If your email service provider offers a spam filter, make use of it. Be aware that some spam is likely to slip past the filter sometimes. Also, don't have the service provider's spam filter automatically delete possible spam – there is always the odd email which you want but which the filter decides is spam. Make sure the spam filter is set up to move the spam to a spam or junk folder, then check it periodically to make sure there isn't something in there you actually want.

Action 2

Treat emails you don't expect with caution. Files attached to such emails and URLs they invite you to click on cannot be trusted.

Action 3

Don't be shy to verify emails that appear to come from your trusted financial institutions by telephone. Look up the telephone number and ignore any that came with the email. While such 'phishing' emails are primarily aimed at identity theft, it's a good bet any website they invite you to visit may try to install some malware for you.

Action 4

Treat offers of enormous or easy financial gain with scepticism. The people sending them are primarily money launderers, but any websites they promote may be toxic.

Action 5

Treat all channels you can use to chat to people with similar caution. Unexpected offers or warnings, even apparently from familiar contacts, should ideally be verified through another channel. You need to be sure you know who you're getting that file from, or whose website you're putting your details into.

Disposable PCs

You may have noticed that, so far, our malware avoidance strategy has only claimed to reduce the risks of acquiring a collection of malware, leaving you hoping that if you do let malware in, your virus and spyware scanners will be able to detect and disable it. If you like surfing the wilder shores of the Internet, the risk can be very high and just reducing it might not make much of a difference – you're going where the malware is, so it's inevitable you'll run into some, and sooner rather than later. If it's something your scanners know about, you'll recover. If it isn't, you may be in trouble.

But if you have a recent, powerful PC and you would be prepared to reinstall Microsoft Windows, then with a little technical effort you can install a second copy of Windows inside your real PC's Microsoft Windows. You can then run your vulnerable browser inside this second copy. This process is called 'running a virtual machine' or just 'virtualisation'. Software emulates the hardware components of a PC, like the disk and CD-ROM drive.

The disk appears as a big file or files, called a 'virtual disk', in your real PC's file system. The other real components of your PC, like the keyboard, mouse, screen and network card, are shared intelligently with the virtual machine, the screen appearing in a window on your Desktop. The virtualised copy of Microsoft Windows can't tell it isn't running on real hardware.

What's the advantage? Your recent, powerful PC will also come with plenty of disk space, so after you install the virtualised Windows, you can back it up simply by copying the real PC file that represents the virtualised Windows hard disk. You can now browse the Web using a browser inside the virtualised Windows, and at the first sign of malware problems, or just whenever you feel like it, you can shut the virtual Windows down and replace the possibly malware-infested version with the backup copy you made of the virtual disk. Restart the virtual machine and you're right back where you were when you installed Windows on it, before the malware arrived. This process isn't instantaneous, but it's a lot quicker than doing a complete install of Microsoft Windows.

There's a performance price to be paid for this virtualisation, and running a virtual machine seems to cost between 10 and 25 per cent of your performance. On recent, powerful PCs, often running multiple core CPUs, you may hardly notice the difference. On less powerful PCs, you may not have enough processing power to make this option viable.

We've had excellent results running the free VMware Server (see Useful Resources). Several other free fully-featured virtualisation products exist as well. More seem to arrive on a frequent basis.

If working out how to install the virtualisation software and putting Microsoft Windows on it seems like a lot of work, consider using the following guide to install Damn Small Linux and VMware Player: http://www.lifehack. org/articles/technology/beginners-guide-run-linux-like-any-other-program-in-windows.html.

In a very short time on a broadband connection, you can be running a Linux virtual machine to browse the Web, safely and securely. Because it's a Linux browser you'll be running, there may be some sites that won't work properly with it.

In fact, there are a large number of virtualisation-based projects available. Anyone who's interested in maximum security should investigate JanusVM (see Useful Resources). This project may require you to come to terms with some advanced networking.

If you decide to take the virtualisation route to avoid malware, you shouldn't ignore protection on your real PC's Microsoft Windows. You still need a firewall, anti-virus and anti-spyware packages on the real PC. It's also a good idea to install these packages on your virtualised Microsoft Windows before you make your 'just installed' backup. Then when you dispose of your old virtual PC and replace it with a fresh version of the copy you made, your new one has all its protection ready installed and you're set to go.

Useful Resources

This section contains resources mentioned in the book and a selection of relevant software packages. Microsoft applications are the most commonly used by home PC users but you may like to try a few alternatives listed here.

Online backup facilities

BT Digital Vault
www.digitalvault.bt.com
BT's offering has suffered some problems, but seems improved now.

Mozy
mozy.com
An American service with a good reputation.

SteekUP
www.steekup.com
A French service, also well regarded.

Security and anti-virus software

Ad-Aware
www.lavasoft.com
One of the most established anti-spyware products on the market. Available in a free version for home use and

there's a more extensive version available that you have to pay for.

AVG Free
free.grisoft.com
This is a nice little free anti-virus package with regular daily updates and full scanning facilities at a price that suits – nothing. The only disadvantage is that anti-virus is all you get for free. If you want facilities like a non-Microsoft firewall, malware and spyware protection and everything else that security software manufacturers offer, you'll have to pay for it like any other package. But if you only use your PC for basic email, surfing and the like, you may find the free version does the trick for you.

Spybot: Search and Destroy
www.safer-networking.org
This is another excellent anti-spyware product and a good candidate for Best Software Product Name. It's free, but if you use it consider making a small donation to help keep it free.

Problem-solving websites and forums
We'd love to list a one-stop problem-solving website, but there are far too many of them. We always start with a search engine (we use Google – www.google.co.uk) to find out where people are talking about a problem, then decide whether the source of the information is credible.

Utility software

7-Zip

www.7-zip.org

A very capable free program for handling archives and compressed files.

DBAN – Darik's Boot and Nuke

dban.sourceforge.net

Does what it says on the tin. Boots up and nukes your PC's hard disks. Good for wiping disks before letting them out of your hands, but use with extreme caution. It nukes every hard disk it can find, so make sure you know what you're doing.

Filezilla

filezilla-project.org

If you need to do any file transferring (e.g. uploading and downloading files to your website), Filezilla is a good, free FTP (File Transfer Protocol) application. It has a good system of managing and connecting to multiple sites and an easy drag-and-drop interface for doing the uploading and downloading.

Internet Owl

www.internetowl.com

A free program which monitors web pages looking for changes. Not all sites provide an RSS feed to keep interested people up to date, and this is a good tool for those websites. You just tell it which pages you want it to keep an eye on, and how often to check, and it does the rest, popping up a little window to notify you when a page changes.

For those who prefer not to run an application on their PC to do this, check out www.changedetection.com, a free web-based service which does the same thing and sends you an email instead when any page changes.

JanusVM

www.janusvm.com

An application which uses VMware (see below) to run a Linux-based high-security Internet filter system on your Windows PC designed to improve your browsing security and privacy.

Memtest86

www.memtest86.com

Download and burn a free, bootable CD which will test your PC's memory and diagnose problems.

MoveOnBoot

This small utility moves or deletes otherwise unmoveable or undeletable files by doing the job before Microsoft Windows has fully booted itself. When files become so undeletable that a reboot doesn't help, MoveOnBoot may do.

VMware Server

www.vmware.com

This application allows you to run 'virtual PCs' on your real PC. A virtual PC is an application which runs a copy of an operating system (like Windows) and makes it think it's running on a real PC all by itself. This is useful for security (running a browser in a virtual PC keeps any security risks isolated within the virtual PC), running different operating systems on the same PC at the same time, or simply running older versions of operating systems (have a game which only runs on Windows 98? Run it in a Windows 98 virtual PC). VMware server is free, although you have to register it, and bigger, flashier versions are available for money (real, not virtual).

Web browsers, email, office and business software

Firefox

www.mozilla.com

Firefox is a good, fast, robust web browser and is completely free. It tends to have fewer security holes than Internet Explorer (though Internet Explorer is improving with each new version). It provides all the features you want in a web browser – tabbed browsing, pop-up blocking, RSS feed reader, search box on the toolbar, spyware protection etc. There are also literally hundreds of add-ons you can install, written by other people who wanted an additional feature or a different look.

If neither Firefox nor Internet Explorer is your cup of tea, among others you could try are Opera, Safari and Netscape.

Thunderbird

www.mozilla.com

Thunderbird is a good email client brought to you by the same people who gave you Firefox, and it too is completely free. If you're looking for something more sophisticated than Outlook Express but don't want to pay for the full version of Outlook, you could do a lot worse than Thunderbird. It does all the standard email things like filtering, spam detection, templates, searches, message tagging and rule processing. Like Firefox, it is a good, robust piece of software, and also has a ton of add-ons you can install. It also has a calendar function (see Lightning below) and a basic but effective task manager.

Open Office
www.openoffice.org
Open Office is a complete replacement for Microsoft Office written by the good folks at Sun Microsystems, but with the distinct advantage that it doesn't cost a bean. It consists of five parts – Writer (word processing), Calc (spreadsheets), Impress (presentations), Draw (graphics and diagrams) and Base (a database). With these you can do anything Microsoft Office does. You can also read any file produced by Microsoft Office and save data to a disk in Microsoft Office format if the person you're sending it to doesn't have Open Office themselves. This book was written in Writer, and then saved as a Word document so our publisher could read it. Who knows, when the editor reads this they might switch to Open Office themselves.

Lightning
www.mozilla.com
Not a separate product as such, but an add-on to Thunderbird to give you full calendar facilities and task management integrated right into Thunderbird. It is also

available as a separate product by the name of Sunbird, but we prefer having it in our email application.

Gnucash

www.gnucash.org
A free accounts package which will handle your personal finances, or if you have a small business, it will cope with that quite well.

Skype

www.skype.com
Just can't recommend this one highly enough. Skype allows you to talk to other people all over the world absolutely free. Well, that's a bit of an overstatement. The software is free, and you can have a text chat (instant messaging) with any other Skype user for free. If you want to chat to them like on a phone, you'll need to get a VOIP (voice over internet) phone or a headset with headphones and a microphone to plug into your PC.

With millions of users, that's a lot of people you can talk to for free. But if your friends are like ours, most of them won't have Skype, so that doesn't really help. However, you can invest some money (how much is up to you) in SkypeOut, which is like pay as you go for mobile phones. The advantage is that you can phone anyone, almost anywhere in the world, for around 1p per minute. In three years of using Skype regularly for international phone calls to the US, Australia and various places in Europe, I still have over £4 left of the original £10 I put into SkypeOut. It's hard to find value like that anywhere.

Glossary

ADSL/ADSL2
Asymmetric Digital Subscriber Line is a technology used to send computer data down a standard phone line without interfering with normal phone use.

application
A computer program which allows you to do something useful.

audit file
See **log**.

AVI
Audio Video Interleaves. A method of compressing video files to a much smaller size.

backup
A copy of computer files in case of problems (**back up** – the act of making the copy).

BIOS
Basic Input/Output System, the program your computer uses to talk to other devices when starting up.

blog
Like an online diary where someone writes down thoughts, ideas and anything else they like so other people can read them.

boot

The process of starting up your PC so it's usable. **Bootable**: a hard drive or CD/DVD you can boot from.

broadband

A method of connecting to the Internet allowing for much higher transfer rates for data. Includes ADSL and cable connections.

browser

An application allowing you to access pages on, and download files from, the Internet.

bug

An error or defect in a computer program.

cable

A method of connecting to the Internet through a cable laid in your street. You can also get television and telephone services over cable.

cache

A copy of something held on another computer which is stored on your PC so it doesn't have to go and ask the other computer for it whenever you want to access it.

CD

A type of optical disk. Originally developed for storing music on as an alternative to vinyl records, these are also now widely used for storing computer programs and data.

client

A program which asks for data from another computer (called the server) and then processes the data. Outlook is an email client which gets email from your mail server and allows you to read, reply etc. Your web browser is a client asking a web server for data (pages) and displaying them for you to read.

cookies

Used by websites to store settings and information in your browser.

CPU

Central Processing Unit, the computer's brain.

database

A collection of data, usually indexed for quick access.

debug

To diagnose and fix computer problems.

directory

See **folder**.

drive

A device for reading and writing data to and from disks.

driver

A special program which allows a computer to talk to another piece of hardware.

DVD
Like a CD, but holds a lot more data.

email
Electronic mail, a way of sending messages to other people using other computers anywhere in the world so quickly that you don't have time to consider what you've said before you say it.

Ethernet
The technology used to implement wired LANs.

filter
A whitelist email filter ensures emails from a list of sources are passed, and everything else is rejected. A blacklist filter rejects all emails from a list of sources and passes everything else. A MAC address filter is a feature on a wireless router that only permits identified PCs to access the wireless network, another example of a whitelist filter.

firewall
A piece of software designed to restrict other computers' access to your computer.

FireWire
An interface for wired high speed transfer of data between two devices. Also known as IEE 1394 and i.LINK.

folder
A logical grouping of files on a computer disk.

forum
An Internet site where people can leave messages and reply to other messages. Sort of like email but anyone can see it and add to or comment on stuff other people have written.

FTP
File Transfer Protocol. A protocol used by two computers to talk to each other and send files back and forth.

firewall
Software which limits who can connect to your PC over the network, so as to increase its security.

function keys
The keys numbered F1 to F12 (sometimes there are more) across the top of your keyboard.

hardware
Any physical bits and pieces which are parts of a computer.

HTML
HyperText Markup Language – the language web pages are written in.

hub
A small device which provides multiple USB sockets and plugs into one USB on the computer.

hyperlink

On a web page, the hyperlinks lead to other web pages when you click on them.

ICT

Information and Communications Technology – computing.

IDE

Integrated Drive Electronics, an interface for PCs to use to communicate with disk drives.

IE

Internet Explorer, Microsoft's web browser.

IM

Instant messenger. An application which allows users to send messages back and forth in real time over the Internet.

IMAP

Internet Message Access Protocol, one of the ways your email client can receive email.

Internet

A network of millions of computers all over the world which can talk to each other. If you're connected to the Internet, your PC is one of the computers which make up this network.

ISP

Internet Service Provider, or just 'service provider'. The company you pay money to provide you with Internet access.

IT

Information Technology – computing.

KVM

Keyboard Video Mouse switch. A device which allows a keyboard, screen and mouse (and sometimes speakers) to be shared between two or more PCs.

LAN

Local Area Network. A small network of computers linked together without needing access to the Internet.

Linux (or GNU/Linux)

An alternative operating system to Windows, much beloved by geeks.

log

A record kept by a program of what it's done and any errors that occurred.

LLU

Local Loop Unbundling. A regulatory process whereby multiple firms can use and install equipment in local telephone exchanges.

MAC

Media Access Control address. A unique ID which identifies a NIC (and thus a computer) on a network.

malware

Any software that maliciously does something undesirable.

memory

Hardware used by the CPU to remember stuff on a temporary basis. Turning the PC off will lose any information held in memory.

menu bar

A bar just underneath the title bar of a window which contains menu items, for example File, Edit, View and Help.

MFD

Multi Function Device. A single device which can act as a printer, scanner, photocopier and sometimes fax machine.

microfilter

A small device which plugs into a normal phone socket and splits the phone and ADSL signals into two separate sockets.

modem
Modulator-demodulator. A device which changes a data signal into tones to send down a phone line and receives tones and changes them back into data for a PC.

network
A group of computers that can talk to each other.

NIC
Network Interface Card. A card which is built into or sometimes just plugs into your computer to give Ethernet networking facilities.

online
Being connected to the Internet. Also used to describe places and resources on the Internet.

(OS) Operating system
A group of computer programs which control everything that happens on a PC enabling you to use it.

package
An alternative name for a software program or more usually several programs bundled together into one installation file.

page
A logical grouping of information on the Internet displayed by a browser.

partition
A method of dividing up one large disk to look to the computer like several smaller disks.

phishing
An attempt to criminally and fraudulently acquire sensitive information by masquerading as a trustworthy entity in an electronic communication.

POP/POP3
Post Office Protocol, one of the ways your email client can receive email.

port
A door in a computer firewall. The firewall can be set up to permit access through the door or not, or to permit access only one way.

RAM
Random Access Memory; see **memory**.

registry
A file used by Windows and applications on a Windows PC to store very important system-related information.

restore
The act of copying data saved in a backup to recover data as it was when the backup was performed.

router

A device which communicates with an ISP providing Ethernet and/or wireless connection to the Internet for multiple computers on a LAN.

RSS

Really Simple Syndication. Provides an easy method to access frequently updated information such as news headlines. You can subscribe to an RSS feed to get summaries of all the latest items.

Safe Mode

A special way of starting Windows which uses a minimum amount of software required to actually get the computer working.

server

See **client**.

software

Programs which run on a computer.

spam

Originally unsolicited commercial email, now widened to include any unwanted electronic communication.

SMTP

Simple Mail Transfer Protocol is used by your email client to send emails.

SSID
Service Set Identifier. A name you give to your wireless network so other computers can locate it.

surf
To use a browser to look at pages on the Internet.

Taskbar
The bar of icons shown at the bottom of a Windows Desktop.

toolbar
A set of icons, usually shown just below the menu bar in an application, giving simple one-click access to commonly used functions.

trojan
A type of virus which comes hidden in another useful piece of software.

update
A set of changes to a program to improve or fix it, and the act of applying those changes.

UPS
Uninterruptible Power Supply, like a huge battery your computer is plugged into in case of general power failure.

URL
Uniform Resource Locator. A unique name identifying a page on the Internet, such as www.google.co.uk.

USB
Universal Serial Bus. A type of plug and socket that is the same between all sorts of computers and devices, meaning every device you want to plug into your computer doesn't have to have a special socket.

utility
A piece of software which performs a single task or small range of tasks, often concerned with managing or tuning operating systems, hardware and other software.

virtual
In computing, virtual is used to mean 'not real' or 'simulated'. Virtualisation software can be used to simulate complete PCs in software.

virus
A program which is passed from one computer to another to do bad things to it. Or at least not good things.

VOIP
Voice Over Internet Protocol. The interface used for allowing voice communication over the Internet.

WEP
Wired Equivalent Privacy. A security system designed to restrict access to a wireless technology. Less secure than WPA.

wired
Connected by wires; not wireless.

wireless
A method of communication between devices and computers using a radio link instead of wires.

worm
A self-propagating piece of malware.

WPA
Wi-Fi Protected Access. A security system designed to restrict access to a wireless technology. More secure than WEP.

zip
A term used to mean a compressed file, or the act of compressing a file.

zombie
A PC that is being controlled remotely by malware which has compromised it.

www.summersdale.com